What I Learned
When I Almost Died

How a Maniac TV Producer

Put Down His BlackBerry

and Started to Live His Life

Chris Licht

Simon & Schuster

New York   London   Toronto   Sydney

Simon & Schuster
1230 Avenue of the Americas
New York, NY 10020

Copyright © 2011 by Chris Licht

First Simon & Schuster hardcover edition May 2011

SIMON & SCHUSTER and colophon are registered trademarks
of Simon & Schuster, Inc.

For information about special discounts for bulk purchases,
please contact Simon & Schuster Special Sales at
1-866-506-1949 or business@simonandschuster.com.

The Simon & Schuster Speakers Bureau can bring authors
to your live event. For more information or to book an event,
contact the Simon & Schuster Speakers Bureau at
1-866-248-3049 or visit our website at www.simonspeakers.com.

Designed by Nancy Singer

Manufactured in the United States of America

10 9 8 7 6 5 4 3 2 1

Library of Congress Cataloging-in-Publication Data

Licht, Chris.
    What I learned when I almost died : how a maniac tv producer put
down his BlackBerry and started to live his life / Chris Licht. —1st Simon
& Schuster hardcover ed.
   1. Licht, Chris. 2. Television producers and directors—United States—
Biography. I. Title.
    PN1992.4.L45A3 2011
    791.4502'33092—dc22
    [B]
    2011011244

ISBN 978-1-4516-2767-1
ISBN 978-1-4516-2768-8 (ebook)

To my family—who make life worth living

Contents

What I Learned
When I Almost Died

The Killer Producer

Lately, if I happen to be looking through my address book for a phone number, I'm apt to stop when I come across the name of someone I haven't been in touch with for a while. A friend, maybe, or an acquaintance. When I do, I'm likely to fire off an e-mail with no more length or gravitas than this:

Hey, how you been?

The gesture is a small one, but I didn't used to do this. Days that were filled with the pressure and crises of running a national cable television program had little room for casual nicety. If I wasn't in the control room producing it, I was in my office thinking about how to produce it. If the talent was unhappy, I'd let it gnaw at my gut. If somebody screwed up, I could go off like a roadside bomb, in a finger snap. I knew this. But the show so consumed me that it couldn't be merely acceptable. It had to be great. I had ambitions. I had to be the killer producer.

Then one day, with no warning whatsoever, I became scary sick in a random and hard-to-figure way, given that I was not even forty years old. Most people with the medical emergency I had do not emerge from the experience physically intact, if they emerge at all. Weeks later, my health restored, I went back to work, and was eager and happy to do so. Illness hadn't scared me into some big life makeover. I had no urge to surrender my spot in the fast lane for ownership of a B&B in Vermont.

But serious illness had recalibrated me. It had brought a trove of knowledge, as if I had involuntarily paid a painful tuition for an elite education. It was about letting go of my fears. It was about what I could control and what I couldn't, and how people felt about me, really felt about me. It was about how to use time. It was even about Joe Biden, the vice president of the United States.

It would be nice, I thought, if everyone could get the education I had gotten without having to nearly die.

So I decided to write a book.

chapter one

The Event

The man who would become my neurosurgeon doubts that a brain can make a noise. Mine did. I'm sure of it. On a cool, partly cloudy spring day not long after nine in the morning, my brain went audible, emitting a *pop* from deep within, not a loud one, more like a balloon had been pricked in the distance.

Now came something else. It was as if a glass of water had tipped up there and spilled its contents; only this didn't feel like a liquid, just a sensation of movement inside, from the back of my head toward the front. Now someone clamped a vise around my skull. Now someone tightened the vise with sadistic gusto, evidently striving for a pain number so far above ten it would merit a Guinness entry.

My body's inventiveness and the speed of its transformation were bewildering, and darkly impressive. In the time it takes to listen to a voice mail, which is what I had been doing, it had mustered a vicious headache. I was having a unique event, which I normally enjoy. Olympics? Worked several, loved them. Super Bowls, World Series, national political conventions, A-list receptions, book parties, movie screenings, all cool. This, absolutely not.

I was suddenly in the bizarre position of thinking about what was going wrong with the thing doing my thinking. My brain was trying to diagnose its own malfunction.

Was this a stroke?

In any television producer's career, especially if he comes up through local news, he usually does enough stories about "Stroke Awareness Month" or similar causes that he comes to know the warning signs by heart. I did. I ran down the list.

Fingers movable?

Yes.

Vision blurred?

No.

Words slurred?

"There's a lot of traffic," I said.

Sounded smooth.

I said this to the only other person around, the driver

of a black Cadillac Escalade into whose rear seat I had dropped a few minutes before, back in my healthy era.

Everything seemed to be working properly except, of course, my head. I knew where I was, on Massachusetts Avenue in Washington. I knew when it was, Wednesday, April 28, 2010. So it seemed reasonable to conclude tomorrow's newspaper would not feature an obituary noting the passing of MSNBC's Christopher A. Licht, 38, husband of Jenny and father of Andrew, twenty months.

Which was comforting, but this still really, really hurt.

In the minutes preceding the pop, I was fine. I had never been an addict, never had surgery, never been rushed to an emergency room, needed no medications, was not overweight, had excellent blood pressure, never smoked, was filled with energy and confidence. Stress? No doubt there was stress. I was in live television, from 6 to 9 A.M. Eastern, five days a week, as the executive producer of a show called *Morning Joe*. Everybody in television has stress. The medium overflows with its ingredients. Money. Egos. Instant ratings. Constant deadlines. But I thrived on being *MJ*'s executive producer.

Having ruled out stroke, I was out of theories. I abandoned voice mail and dialed for help. Not to my wife, because telling her about the vise gripping my head without knowing why it was doing so would upset her without of-fering solace. Jenny has no medical background; like me, she's in television. And she was in New York City, where we live, and could hardly swing by in a few minutes to commiserate in the back of this SUV. I called Dad.

Peter Licht is a doctor, an internist. He and my mother, Susan, who is a physician's associate, work in the same medical office and still live in the house in Connecticut where I grew up with my sister, Stephanie. Until now, I had never called either parent about a medical emergency that I myself was suffering. But Dad is a man of no bull and no drama, and he never coddles and never overreacts. Once, in my teens, at camp in Florida, I took a tumble while barefoot waterskiing and damaged an eardrum. A local doctor prescribed major pain meds, really serious stuff. Dad declared this was nonsense, take two aspirin. If my super-headache was nothing, he'd say so. If it was something, he'd say that.

Dad didn't answer his cell. I called the house.

Mom was surprised I was in Washington because mostly we're in New York, at 30 Rockefeller Center, 30 Rock. But Washington is where our nation keeps its na-tional politicians and politics is MJ's métier, so we take the show there often. Not thirty minutes earlier, we had wrapped up the day's version and the Escalade had started back to my hotel from NBC's Washington bureau. The show's hosts, Mika Brzezinski and Joe Scarborough, were off to a speech.

"Something's wrong with me," I said to Mom.

I described the sensations. She was mildly concerned. As well as anyone, she knew I was never sick.

"It probably wouldn't hurt to go to the hospital."

She got a second call from me a few minutes later.

"I gotta tell you, my neck is starting to get stiff."

I was beginning to have trouble moving my head in any direction, in addition to having pain. I couldn't even lean it against the seat. Mom became more insistent.

"I think you should go to the hospital."

Five minutes later, it was Dad calling.

"You need to go to the emergency room and you need to get a CAT scan, and I'm telling you that when you get there, you need to tell them you do not get headaches and this is the worst headache of your life."

He was not panicked, because he never is. He was firm.

"Okay, good," I said.

My response must have been too casual.

"Say that to me," he said. "You do not get headaches and this is the worst headache of your life. Say that exactly."

"I do not get headaches and this is the worst headache of my life."

"Call me when you know what's going on."

Dad didn't suspect anything specific; nor was he terribly worried. After all, I was conscious and coherent. What he wanted was that CAT scan, because that would be hard data, not a guess or a supposition. As for his pointed instruction to say "never get headaches" and "worst of my life," I didn't know, and didn't ask, but that is an informal code within the medical profession. Any decent emergency room would interpret the phrases to mean I was not a habitual complainer, I was in the midst of something rare, pay attention, give me a CAT scan.

Having visited Washington so often, I knew where I wanted to go—George Washington University Hospital in the neighborhood known as Foggy Bottom. They took President Ronald Reagan there when he was shot in 1981, a good enough endorsement as far as I was concerned. And it was a short distance from my hotel. In all probability, they would give me something to knock down the pain and I would cycle back to my room and get on with the day. There was another show tomorrow to prep for, because there always is another show to prep for, and there was a black-tie dinner that night featuring Bill Clinton and Bono. Mika and Joe were the hosts. I was going.

Nothing traumatic had marred my life to that moment, and there was no reason to think the streak would end. Job, wife, kid, health, all good. Pessimism was not my default position. Setback happened to the other guy, not me.

"Can we go to the GW emergency room?" I said to the driver.

We were already headed in that direction. But while the busiest part of my day had ended when MJ did, the busiest of Washington's was still unfolding. Traffic was thick. This was bad. My head was being squeezed without intermission, and now the landscape was only crawling past. Here's the National Cathedral. Here's Rock Creek Park. Here's a bunch of embassies. At one point, we inched past the grounds of the U.S. Naval Observatory, the vice president's official residence. In a couple of hours, its occupant and I were going to have a bond.

By now I had new sensations. My head was pulsing with each heartbeat, and each pulse made the hurt worse. My stomach was nauseous and I was trying mightily not to throw up. I was sweating. At some point, I asked if there were any shortcuts, but there were none.

I still didn't envision the horrible, like disability or death, and wasn't having anguished thoughts about Jenny and Andrew. But I wanted to get to the hospital and be given something to make the pain evaporate. It was making concentration so difficult that listening to more voice mails or making more calls was impossible.

Finally, we rolled up to the stone facade of George Washington. I told the driver to wait, because I suspected I would be back momentarily, and I gingerly took my head up two flights of steps, through the pedestrian entrance of the emergency room, to a counter where a woman sat. She was the "Greet Tech."

"I'm having a real problem here," I said.

Greet Tech said something noncommittal, like "yup." My father's words found my lips.

"I do not get headaches, I never get headaches, and I'm having the worst headache of my life. There's something very wrong with me. And I need to see somebody now."

Greet Tech came to life. She knew the code, even if I didn't.

"I believe you are in the right place," she said.

She wanted identification. There were forms.

Then, I sat.

The reception area was not empty. Decades passed. My hands cradled my head and there arose from me a kind of low moan, an "ahhh," because I sincerely hurt, and if that drew a little attention, great. It was actually only minutes before they beckoned me to a triage cubicle, where a nurse checked my vitals and found them normal except for blood pressure, which stood at 159 over 107.

They dropped me in a wheelchair and rolled me through double doors and into the heart of the emergency room, to a small examination bay that was all fluorescence and monitoring equipment. I knew such bays. I'd been to ERs as a kid with Dad, sometimes playfully hooked up to EKGs by the nurses.

My bay was curtained into halves, front and back, and each had a bed with wheels and rails. They rolled me to the back, making me the patient in C2B. Patient C2A, a woman, seemed to have fallen during a footrace that morning. I never did get the story. They told me to get undressed, put on one of those haute couture hospital gowns, and put my street clothes in a clear, plastic bag.

Now I remembered that not a soul beyond the confines of the hospital knew where I was.

Dad and Mom had told me to get to an emergency room, but they didn't know which one I'd chosen. Nobody at *Morning Joe* even knew I was having a mini-nightmare. Jenny didn't. Things had unraveled so quickly. It hadn't even been an hour since the show ended. At 9:59 A.M., I sent a text to Mika Brzezinski at the Marriott Wardman Park hotel, the site of her and Joe's speech.

In er at gw

Got excruciating and sudden pain in head

Scared—getting cat scan

Will call when I can

I wasn't scared, really. The word was only meant to get her attention. Joe and Mika needed to know their executive producer was going to be out of touch and the reason wasn't trivial. But my goal wasn't to herald a huge personal emergency. Everything in my past said this would be a brief suspension of duty. The EP would be getting out of George Washington.

chapter two

The Little Anchor

There once was a boy with a camera in a house on a sylvan hill in Connecticut.

I was eleven. The camera was a clunky old VCR sort because this was 1983. I set it up in the basement TV room, where I had a desk, and on the desk I put a microphone on a tiny stand.

Each week, I would write a script and put on my tweed sport coat, a dress shirt and a tie, but no dress slacks, because the camera would show me only from the waist up, so underpants were okay. My hair was often an unruly mop, but in every other way I was the mature, authoritative preteen host of *The Week in Review,* the leading and only show on the WBC television network, which I owned and all of whose viewers were named Licht.

The show was thorough, covering national and international news, local items, sports, obits, weather, and pop culture. Sometimes it featured my sister, Stephanie, who was nearly three years younger and reluctant, or I'd bring in Dad for medical reports and sports commentary. (He was versatile.) If Stephanie screwed up or didn't take the show seriously, the host could get miffed. At times, I had to bribe her for an appearance or to work the camera, once offering a Velcro Michael Jackson wallet. Mom and Dad still have the show tapes.

Anchor:

For some people, the world is just one big fuzzy thing. Let The Week in Review *focus it in for you.* (The screen image morphs from hazy and indistinct to a knife-sharp map of the seven continents.)

We'll be back right after these messages with why we have two feet of snow on the ground. (Cut to commercials, real ones I had taped off TV and spliced in.)

This is Chris Licht speaking. Join us next week. (Run credits.)

It wasn't a coincidence that my network's name was one letter away from NBC. I loved NBC. When I was little, the Lichts took the 30 Rock tour, and our gaggle of the bug-eyed was taken into a studio, where the tour guides asked for volunteers to play Johnny Carson and

Ed McMahon. Up went my hand. They made me Johnny and made some older guy Ed, put us in chairs, and gave us a script to read. The older guy was terrible. I was so good my own mother couldn't believe it. I had Johnny down cold.

One summer when I was nine or so, we rented a condo on Martha's Vineyard. Carl Stern was renting nearby. Carl was an NBC star, covering the U.S. Supreme Court and the Justice Department, winning numerous awards. Mom says I stuck like glue to the guy. About a month after we got back from vacation, the phone rang at our house.

Dad picked up.

It was Carl Stern.

"Just returning Chris's call."

On the Vineyard, Carl had given me his number, probably secure in the thought that no nine-year-old would actually call a leading national television correspondent. But I did, because I felt Carl and I had much to discuss, being in the same business. I used to call Sue Simmons, too, one of the anchors of WNBC–New York's evening news. I called Sue a lot, enough to become known to her as "Chris from Connecticut." Mom says I once told Sue, "I'm going to work for NBC one day." (Years later, my wife worked with Sue at WNBC, and mentioned to her that she was dating someone Sue knew, someone who used to telephone her as a kid. "Chris from Connecticut?" Sue said.)

As my childhood fascination with broadcasting grew, I pictured myself as some kind of network "talent," an anchor perhaps, certainly a reporter, a person on the air. When I went off to Syracuse University to study broadcasting, Stephanie handwrote a letter assuring her big brother, *You're going to be in Tom Brokaw's seat one day.*

I might have had the voice for it. In the wee hours on weekends during high school, I earned four dollars an hour as a DJ on a fifty-thousand-watt rock station that blanketed Connecticut. This made me a bit of a celebrity among my peers, especially female, and I'd dedicate songs to my buddies who were out doing what more normal teenage males did on weekend nights, which was hang out. If you had been listening, my best friend Marc Nespoli says, you would have assumed from the dulcet pipes that I "was thirty, not eighteen."

After graduating from Syracuse, I settled in Allentown, Pennsylvania, to commence my television news ascent. The job there, working for a company that produced and sold medical stories that television stations could air as their own, was instructive and decent. But life in Allentown was slow death in obscurity.

So when a friend suggested I move to Los Angeles to help with his production company, I leaped at the chance to work for nothing, which is what they paid me for the first couple of months. In time, I was working on a television pilot two floors above the newsroom of KNBC, the local NBC-owned station, and I would hang out down there, doing research if asked. I liked the energy of a newsroom. And there I got to know Jeff Kaufman.

In the summer of 1995, Jeff was the executive producer of a nightly program about the trial of one Orenthal James Simpson, who was charged with the knife murders of his ex-wife and a friend of hers. With its threads of sex, race, violence, and police bias, the O.J. trial was big. You might have heard of it. Jeff's live half-hour program recapped each day's testimony, beginning at 7:30 P.M. One day, he asked if I wanted a full-time job as one of the show's writers.

I didn't know how to write television copy, but that was a minor matter I kept to myself. This was a big show in a big city about big news. I accepted. Jeff butchered nearly every sentence I wrote during my early days, and I got schooled.

The O.J. show was supervised each night by a certain line producer, except on Wednesdays, when he left early to teach a college class. He would designate a writer to sit in his chair during the show, which was not as big a risk as it sounds, because the trial always ended at five, giving us plenty of time to prepare for seven-thirty before he left. To be Line Producer for a Day was a babysitting job, a judgment-free exercise, so easy that one evening they gave the chore to me.

Then, at 6:15 P.M., with the line producer now gone and Jeff off that day, the Fuhrman tapes were released.

Mark Fuhrman was a detective with the Los Angeles Police Department who investigated the O.J. case. He is white. Simpson is black. Fuhrman's racial attitudes were a major part of the defense's case because Simpson's lawyers believed the police were prejudiced against their client. Fuhrman had sworn in court he held no racial animus and hadn't used the word *nigger* in a decade.

But during taped interviews in recent years with a writer developing a screenplay about police officers, Fuhrman had used that very word several dozen times, and now the court had released some of the tapes, which the jury would be allowed to hear.

That detonated our script. There had to be a rewrite. A camera crew had to scramble to get to the home of Fred Goldman, the father of Nicole Simpson's murdered friend, so we could get his reaction to this development that was so damaging to the prosecution's case. That evening's program would be no babysitting affair. I was in charge, me, age twenty-three, training wheels still on and, at that moment, terrified.

With major help from another writer whom I thank to this day, the overhaul of the script came together. But would the camera crew get to Fred Goldman's place in time? The show began. The crew arrived at Goldman's. It began setting up. Five minutes left in the show. Three. There! We went live from the Goldman home, with two minutes to spare.

The adrenaline rush was nothing like I had ever felt. The show was so good that when we had finished, the news director wanted to thank the brilliant soul who had led the effort. He refused to believe it was the Syracuse kid. In fact, he was annoyed I had been put in charge in the first place.

That night changed everything. No more Tom Brokaw. No more aiming to be in front of a camera.

I knew instantly that the feeling of control and creation I had experienced made me happy. I liked sculpting the chaos. To have a vision and see it broadcast on TV, well, there was nothing better than that, I thought. Being on-air talent could not possibly be as wonderful, because you only command the slice of the whole involving you. Being a producer meant having the entire show in your hands.

We all went to a restaurant and got drunk to celebrate.

Producing was what I wanted.

chapter three

A Migraine Guy

Not long after my text entered cyberspace on its way to Mika Brzezinski, a doctor came to my cubicle in the emergency room of George Washington University Hospital and asked me to hold out my arms, push my fists against her hands, and other tasks to discern whether my very disagreeable brain was still in clear communication with the rest of me. She was calm, if detached.

"Look, you're not exhibiting any signs of anything neurologically wrong with you," she said after a few minutes of this, "and I think what you're experiencing is a stress migraine. Do you have a stressful job?"

I told her my job at *MJ*. It was pretty clear she had never heard of the show.

"Well, we're going to get you something for the pain,

and then when I come back, I'm going to give you some tips on how to manage your stress."

"So I'm not going to get a CAT scan?"

"No, you don't need a CAT scan."

A migraine made sense. My nausea had faded, and there were no other symptoms. No fever, and nothing was numb, immobile, or weak. And migraines can be extremely discomforting, and I certainly was extremely discomforted. A migraine this must be.

The satisfaction of a diagnosis was tempered almost immediately by the knowledge that migraines are not one-and-done. In time, there's another, then another, now and forever. How annoying, I thought. I'm now a migraine guy. Who wants membership in this club?

The doctor left. But soon a woman in a black polo shirt came in. The shirt had writing on the back, like TRAUMA TEAM or TRAUMA UNIT, I can't remember. An entirely different aura surrounded her, one of great urgency. She ran through similar neurological tests. I would soon be a leading American authority on those tests.

"Mr. Licht," she said, "I'm going to give you a shot for the pain. Then we're going to take you down and get you a CAT scan."

I read nothing into it. They were merely being safe

about their migraine hypothesis. Anyway, Dad had said to get a scan, so this was good.

What I didn't know was that the doctor in charge of the morning shift in the emergency room had been told the migraine diagnosis for the patient in C2B and thought my problem might be something else. With any patient in the ER, the supervisor's job is to consider the worst possibilities, and she was troubled by the swift, devastating onset of my pain. She wanted more tests and had ordered a nurse to my room with pain medication.

Black Polo gave me the shot. Now down the hall I went to get the CAT scan, which took no time at all, and now back I came to C2B. It was nearly 11 A.M.

In the midst of all this, a text had arrived on my Black-Berry.

Shall I call Jenny?

It was Mika. But I was no longer tethered to my phone. I had turned it off and dumped it into the plastic bag with my clothes, a sign of just how awful my head was feeling, because I never put myself out of reach of the known world. Normally, Mr. BlackBerry and I were conjoined twins.

Mika got no reply.

She texted again, a minute later.

I am sending Louis. And telling Joe when he gets offstage.
We need to hear from you or we will be there.

Again, silence.

At the Marriott Wardman Park, where Joe was about to start his speech, Mika had not read my initial text as conveying a minor, if somewhat unusual, problem. She has tremendous instincts about situations and people and had gotten a dark feeling from my text, which only got darker when she received no answer to hers. She didn't tell Joe; he was about to take the stage.

"Louis, I think we have a serious problem."

Louis Burgdorf, who more or less pummeled me into hiring him after he graduated from college a couple of years ago, is Mika's and Joe's personal aide, and he is usually at their side when they make an appearance.

"I'll stay with Joe," she told him. "We'll do the speech. I want you to go to the hospital."

And now, a ride on the Washington Metro later, he came down a hall of the emergency room as I stood there waiting to use a bathroom. Seeing him was a big comfort. Migraine diagnosis or not, this was no fun.

When we got back to C2B, I climbed aboard my hospital bed and perched there in my goofy gown, which was not what I was wearing when Louis last saw me earlier in the day. He was concerned that there were no nurses, doctors, or technicians, and that I was in such distress and looked so pale.

"My head hurts," I told him. "You don't know. I feel like someone's stabbing me."

To illustrate, I ran my fingertips from the front of my head to the back.

Now Louis's phone was getting short Mika bursts.

What is happening?

Have you heard anything?

Where is Chris? Has he seen a doctor?

????

Whether or not I mentioned the migraine diagnosis to Louis, I can't remember. There's a lot about that day I can't remember. But there wasn't much definitive to tell the outside world in any case. We were still awaiting my CAT-scan results, even if I still thought I had nothing but a migraine. I did ask Louis to call Jenny in New York, because talking to her myself seemed to require far more clarity and concentration than I was likely to have.

Minutes passed. More minutes passed. It seemed as if the hospital had forgotten about C2B. In reality, getting a CAT scan evaluated and uploaded to a hospital's computer system can take time, depending on the demand and the severity of the cases within the emergency room, which, at George Washington, has three dozen patient cubicles. Its emergency room sees seventy-two thousand patients a year, nearly two hundred a day, the second greatest volume in Washington.

At last, a doctor came in.

A new one.

$$\left[\text{ chapter four }\right]$$

Captain Intense

On April 3, 2007, the University of Tennessee defeated Rutgers University to capture the NCAA women's basketball championship, and the next morning Don Imus declared on his national radio show that the losing team's players, most of them African-American, were tattooed, rough, "nappy-headed hos." His CBS show died a short time later.

Imus's suicide-by-slur left MSNBC, the cable network, with a Grand Canyon in its morning lineup. Even though Imus had worked for CBS radio, he had done his show at MSNBC's studios in Secaucus, New Jersey, enabling the network to simulcast it, as easy a way to fill three hours as there is. Now he was gone, but the three hours remained, waiting to be filled by . . . Nobody knew.

On a rainy afternoon in the midst of this uncertainty, as I worked in my apartment in New York, in the room that would become Andrew's after he was born the following year, Joe Scarborough called.

"This Imus stuff is crazy," he said.

At the time, we were doing *Scarborough Country*, a nightly, hour-long collection of politics and pop culture in prime time on MSNBC. Its future seemed uncertain, because the network was starting to slant leftward in the evenings and Joe is a conservative former Republican congressman from Pensacola, Florida.

"I've just sent you a PDF," he said, "and I want to do this."

The PDF attachment to his e-mail contained a proposal for a unique news show that would slide into the vacant Imus slot. It would not offer a conventional morning buffet of fashion, food, and weight-loss tips spliced with twelve-year-olds plucked out of wells or teen-actor graduates of the Betty Ford Clinic. It would serve witty, nonideological conversation among smart guests about politics, business, and culture. Above all, it would exude intelligence. Willie Geist, who became one of its hosts along with Mika and Joe, came to call it "Fantasy Breakfast" because the sharpest minds you can imagine show up at your house for eggs and issues.

Signing off on Joe's idea, Phil Griffin, who was then senior vice president of NBC News, offered a piece of advice. Joe ought to bring me from *Scarborough Country* as his executive producer. In the few years the show had been alive, Joe had chewed through several producers, but he and I had meshed, so much so that Joe says I scrubbed away his reputation around the network as a difficult piece of work.

Joe wants a producer who's organized, has vision, and gets the impossible done. He wants someone with "rocket fuel" in his veins. He wants a killer. I like to think I fit all the criteria. A killer producer never takes no for an answer. A killer relentlessly pushes to land the guest who seems too tough to get, pushes his team to make each segment shine more than the one before, pushes the hosts and himself, pushes every problem toward solution. He does not allow anyone within the building or beyond its walls to thwart him or the show. Hell no. We're *Morning Joe*. Don't tell me I cannot have what I need. I need a yes.

Not long before my brain episode, a reporter from GQ captured me in action pretty well. During a *Morning Joe* one day, Mika and Joe were supposed to talk with Hillary Clinton by satellite, but CNN's morning host, John Roberts, was interviewing her by satellite, too, right before us, and he was running long. The GQ reporter picked up the scene in our control room:

"I'm gonna fucking punch John Roberts myself," says Licht. "Fuck, they're giving it to us a minute and a half late. Fucking assholes." He instructs another producer to tell Fox News, where Hillary is going next, that she may be a bit late, "because unlike CNN, I'm not a douchebag!" Then he starts flipping out because there's only one feed from Haiti and it's going to the freaking Today *show.*

As a result of that little episode, by the way, we have a new rule: no reporters in the control room.

One summer, Joe's twenty-one-year-old son, Joey, was an intern on the third floor of 30 Rock, where *Morning Joe* lives, and after a while Joe asked if Joey had formed any impressions of me.

"Oh, Chris is great," Joey replied. "He's great."

"Well," Joe said, "I've heard that he can be an asshole. That's the word people use."

"In the control room," Joey said, "Chris *is* an asshole. But you need that. There is so much chaos going on in there."

Control Room 3A is a few dozen feet down the hall from the gentility of the *Morning Joe* set. It is my domain. It is not always genteel. It is a dark, low-hanging universe of dozens upon dozens of flat-screen monitors; of consoles and headsets and fatigue and snap decisions; of telephones, jumbo coffees, and chatter, which can morph into shouts, profane shouts, if a teleprompter freezes or Mika's mike is left on during a commercial break or a guest is sonorous. A dialect is spoken in 3A, but it is only tangentially English, things like "We're about thirty heavy" or "Animate now to the hard out."

This is live television, the most difficult kind, because the first take is the only one. The planned sequence of segments is a malleable thing because we may drop a guest as we go, we may add one, we may be surprised by what one says, we may have breaking news, we may lose a satellite feed, we may change songs leading into commercial, we may have to remind those on the set what to say or what not to.

They are the most fun hours of my day. To stand in the shower and come up with an idea for that morning's show and see it take shape is the legal high of being an executive producer. So is opting in midshow to try to hunt down a traveling congressman for a live shot and pulling it off; whispering in Joe's earpiece and hearing the nugget come out of his mouth seconds later; keeping those on the set cool and calm while we in the control room douse a metaphorical fire.

Each day, however, I make hundreds of decisions that go far beyond the mere technical challenges of running a

control room. While I get a huge amount of help from the
MJ team, particularly my senior staff, the buck stops with
me. In large part, I assembled the small, dedicated team
that puts out the show each day. If a controversy brews up
because of something said on the air, damage control falls
to me. If a newspaper calls to check out a rumor about the
show, I have to weigh how to handle it. I make sure the
mix of guests is stimulating and smart. If I have doubts
about the authenticity of a news item we're about to air,
I hold it, which I did recently regarding unsubstantiated
reports a black employee of the U.S. Department of Agri-
culture had been fired for racist remarks. I wanted confir-
mation from the Obama administration, which we got and
aired, a decision that left Joe pretty pleased because unlike
others, we hadn't jumped to any conclusions.

At its core, the look and feel of *Morning Joe* reflects
collaboration among Joe, Mika, and me. One of us will
have an idea for a segment. We'll massage it, play with it,
add elements until, by the end, it's tough to pin down au-
thorship. More than anything, I try to keep Joe's original
vision fresh, to turn his sparks into cutting-edge television,
to stay inside his head.

As the 2010 midterm elections approached, for example, I wanted to do something special on the day after the

balloting. Why not, I thought, do the show from Studio 8H, the biggest at 30 Rock and the home of *Saturday Night Live*? Joe and Mika and our guests could sit on the stage before a live studio audience, which is what *SNL* always has but which morning shows rarely do. Using such a legendary venue would be an electric way of saying the election was a grand, historic event—and we're the team to tell you about it. It would create buzz for us. And it did. People were clamoring for tickets. The *New York Times* took note.

Mike Barnicle, a former newspaper columnist in Boston and a regular on the show, calls me "Captain Intense," possessed of a demonic desire to make *MJ* work. As a journalist, you want to expose problems and make things better. It sounds self-aggrandizing, and probably is, but *MJ* does that. It's part of the solution. They watch at the White House; I know they do, because I get their e-mails. In the jargon of journalism, *MJ* can "drive the day," meaning other news outlets pursue our insights or revelations.

I suppose I could be vice president of programming for the All-Reality Network, if there was one, and make huge piles of cash dreaming up *Dancing with Convicts* or *Who Wants to Marry a Refugee?* I could do that, but I would never want to. Getting up at 4 A.M. to do *MJ* each day, I don't have to hold my nose.

But most of us, if we're honest, are more than our noble ideals. Like most, I nurse ambitions, large ones. I like being a player on a big stage. It's why I love New York City and did not like Allentown, Pennsylvania. I like to be at the core of news and sporting events and sophisticated gatherings, going places and doing things others can't. Doing *MJ* puts me at the center of the big conversation. It's a super-relevant existence.

I lived the show. I gave 100 percent, which means I was always shy a few percentage points to give to family. In retrospect, I know my obsession came at Jenny's expense. She didn't have all of me when I was at home. She almost never had a weekend with me that was not carved up by the BlackBerry, always the BlackBerry.

As our newborn was being taken to be circumcised, I was on the phone doing *MJ* work, obviously not fully in the moment of fresh fatherhood. Why did I even have it on? I skipped the wedding of one of my best friends because it was Sweeps Week. That failure is one of my all-time regrets, but it was an easy call at the time.

A mere three days after Andrew's birth, I went back to work. The 2008 Democratic National Convention was under way in Denver and I was disappointed I couldn't go because of the baby, so I worked double shifts at 30 Rock to help the coverage from there. The next week, I was off to the Republican convention in St. Paul, Minnesota, leaving Jenny alone in the first days of motherhood.

There were other problems, deeper and more wrenching. This part is not easy.

Anyone who meets me probably concludes I am not the retiring type but rather someone who is worldly, comfortable with command, comfortable around powerful people, and skilled in a television studio. All of that is true. But much of the time these past years, my stomach was an emotionally ensnarled place, a big knot.

I was not entirely sure where I stood at work. And I feared that my golden existence at the nexus of substantive and exciting things might end.

Doing a long, live, and barely scripted show every weekday doesn't leave a lot of time for politeness and praise from the talent, Mika and Joe. Snap, do this now. Snap, don't do that again. Snap, go away. There are eruptions of anger, and people stay mad for a while, and there are screwups.

Though Mika found me "a damn good producer," I constantly craved reassurance. She thought I was headed for a meltdown, because I was racked with so much worry about whether she and Joe were happy and about whether there was anything else I needed to be racked with worry about. That's why I worked so much, believing that is what I had to do to make sure everything was all right, and that I was in Joe and Mika's good graces. That angst is common among executive producers, but knowing this was no help to me.

While I was pretty sure Joe considered me indispensable, I was nervous, looking over my shoulder, trying to shield myself and see where I stood in the firmament of NBC. To a degree, Joe says, all ambitious guys do that because we want to keep moving up. We gauge our position in the footrace. But sometimes Joe couldn't tell if my proffered opinion about something reflected my true feeling or a safe one. Often, I covered my ass, out of fear.

If you love what you do, as I did, the thought of not doing it can be scary. For me, the fear was not about losing a paycheck. If they kicked me to the street, I'd land on my feet, because talent is always in demand. Instead, not being Joe and Mika's executive producer was a scary notion because I would no longer be part of that big conversation I mentioned.

Solely because of *Morning Joe*, I had become friendly with Jack Welch, the former chief executive of General Electric, which until recently was NBC's parent company.

He had been advising me about my career. Would such a relationship have ever developed if I had stayed in local television? Probably not. Would it continue if I was no longer with MJ? Unlikely. If fired, I might wind up out of the loop at some backwater news show for nonplayers, the failures. That was my fear.

It's no surprise, then, that in the rhythm of our day, I could go volcanic, firing off profanity-infused e-mails to those below me, often about minor things. I picked fights, too, just to mark territory. I had been working on being less prickly. Welch had told me to give more hugs if I wanted to keep doing big things, and I had been. But self-rehab is a long, slow process.

On the morning of April 28, 2010, I was about to unload on someone in my usual way. I was listening to a voice mail on my BlackBerry about MSNBC's transportation arrangements for the White House Correspondents' Association dinner in Washington, three days away. We had a big table at the dinner, which is the journo-politico meal of the year. The voice mail blathered on about which of our big names would get which drivers to take them to and from the dinner.

It was already a bad day; Joe and I had had a disagreement during the show, a testy one, about camera angles.

Mika had even written Joe a note while they were on the air saying, *Take it easy on the guy*. Now came this silly, silly issue. Cars. Drivers.

Why am I getting a phone call about this? Do people know how much bigger stuff I have to deal with? Does anybody know what I have to put up with?

I would have called someone about the nonsense. I would have dropped a generous dollop of profanity upon them in my dismissive, asshole way.

I would have.

But my brain went *pop*.

chapter five

Free Fall

The new doctor, the one who had just arrived in my cubicle, was Ryanne Mayersak, and she was in her fourth year as an emergency-room attending physician, the supervisor in charge of the other doctors during a shift. Actually, this was her second visit to me. The first had come after Migraine Doctor left but before Louis arrived, and Dr. Mayersak had done neurological tests on me similar to those everybody else had done or would do. She had even given me her educated guess about what my CAT scan would show.

I have no memory of her initial visit. It is a reflection of how badly things unfolded in the next few moments that my brain wound up deleting an entire encounter with a doctor who was giving critical information.

As she entered for what I thought was the first time,

Dr. Mayersak saw I now had a visitor, and she assumed he was not family. (Louis had gotten as far into the ER as he had by saying he was my cousin.) Doctors don't usually give sensitive information to anyone but the patient and his relatives. I told her not to worry about Louis.

"Whatever you have to say, say it."

She delivers a lot of bad news in the emergency room and has found that the best route is not an oblique one, but straight ahead. A patient needs to start processing it, adapting to it, and thinking of questions about it. There I lay on the hospital bed, waiting.

"We've looked at your CAT scan," Dr. Mayersak said, "and you have a significant amount of bleeding in your brain."

A word apparently swam into my consciousness, a word with the impact of a dropped anvil, because Dr. Mayersak thinks this exchange may have happened next:

"Do I have an aneurysm?"

"That's possible."

I couldn't breathe.

Most of us don't know the causes of aneurysms or their treatment, and I certainly didn't, but I knew right away I was in deep trouble. Blood had escaped from my arterial system and into the enormously constricted spaces of my skull, squeezing the most vital organ we have. Blood was causing my headache. Blood might still be leaking.

I fought tears.

There's a well-worn aphorism that all too often we don't recognize the crucial moments until much later, as they recede in the rearview mirror. This one had announced itself with a jackboot to the gut. In this antiseptic, windowless room, in this big Washington hospital, with Louis standing there but my wife and son in New York, my life was pivoting toward a new compass point. I had free-ranging blood in my brain. There was no way I would come out of this the same.

Just a short time earlier, I had been doing a national television show in perfect health. Then, after experiencing sharp pain, I had been safely diagnosed with a migraine. I was out of there. I was done with the hospital. While migraines are unpleasant, I had been told things were, if not fine, then manageable. Now they were very much not fine, they were dangerously wrong. It was like being tricked.

"This is a critical situation," Dr. Mayersak said.

I was in the right place, she said. You'll get the best care. The neurological team had been paged and was on its way and would answer my questions. If I had any right now, she could try to help. The question I came up with reflected the condition of a man whose circuits were being scrambled by profound distress, because it was so deeply trivial and dumb.

"So you're admitting me?"

New thoughts came. I clearly hadn't died, but people with aneurysms don't walk out of hospitals the next day. We're just getting started here. More was coming. My schedule, all those places I had to be and people I had to see, all confidently recorded in the BlackBerry that now slept in the clear plastic bag, had been blown up and re-placed by the unknown.

My immediate future would be here, in this hospital. The master of Control Room 3A had no control in C2B. He could not fix the problem he faced, because this was not the familiar terrain of live television but a place where he was dependent upon neurologists who were coming to treat him and he had no idea how that was done. How could this be happening? Don't they know I am exempt from this sort of thing?

It was the greatest shock of my life.

Not since pneumonia sent my son to an emergency room when he was seven weeks old had I felt as powerless. Actually, I felt more powerless than I did then. I wasn't an observer here, as I was when Andrew was hospitalized. It was me in the bed this time, not me standing beside it. My brain, my future.

To Dr. Mayersak, Louis looked more stunned than I did. He had imagined his producer was merely suffering from too much coffee or too few vitamins, and would be up and on his way. Louis's stomach had dropped at the mention of bleeding, in part because he had been working at NBC's Washington bureau on the day in 2008 when *Meet the Press* host Tim Russert had collapsed and died. Now Louis roped his emotions back into place.

"You're going to be okay, Chris," he said. "I promise. You're going to be okay."

"I know. I'm just scared. This is really scary."

He reached out and took my hand.

"Thanks, man."

"Breathe," he said.

$\left[\text{\textit{chapter six}}\right]$

The Superheroes

At the Marriott Wardman Park hotel, as I learned later, Mika seized Joe's arm as he stepped off the stage, his speech now done. In three years together on the air, Mika and Joe have had quite a few low points and tribulations, but he had never seen the depth of apprehension now sketched on her face.

"We have to go," she said. "Louis says Chris has an aneurysm."

"Chris has a brain aneurysm? Our Chris?"

"Yes, our Chris. We have to go now."

In the car to George Washington, Joe kept repeating his disbelieving question, "Our Chris?" Otherwise, they rode in paralyzed silence. Mika thought the news could kill Joe. She thought the aneurysm could kill me. She saw me as so chronically healthy and resilient, no matter how much she and Joe got on my case about decisions or miscues. Now my head was way wrong. She was speeding to a hospital where things might not end well. People die of this.

Mika Brzezinski, on the outside, has a kind of crazed diva vibe. She is the daughter of Zbigniew Brzezinski, who was President Jimmy Carter's national security adviser, and she is hard-nosed, funny, and a fanatical worker, racing among a high-adrenaline job, two young daughters, a husband who works in television, books she writes and speaking engagements, and somewhere in there she sleeps but never for long. A former CBS network reporter and anchor, she has a deep grounding in television news.

On the inside, no one is more caring. No one will bust down more walls if they need busting. Jenny calls Mika a tornado. We call her "Mommy," because she makes everything all right.

Joe Scarborough is much harder to read, more closed. Though he left Congress in 2001 after more than three terms in the House, he is still a politician who has flawless sensors and total recall of names, events, songs, and dates and perhaps still a politician's wariness.

There's no one more adept at detecting the glimmer of a rising political force or the stench of a loser. Joe has genius instincts for what makes good TV, right down to camera angles and set design, even though he has no background in such. If he could both host his show and run it from Control Room 3A, he would do so and he would be superb at both.

We are The Trifecta, Mika says, though I fully understand they matter more than I. With the success of the show, they have become a brand, serving as masters of ceremonies at dinners and making speeches across the country, and I help push and polish the brand, as well as execute the show they want. They are always in my thoughts. They might have assistants who worry about the details of their travel arrangements and their engagements, but if something goes wrong in their professional lives, it eventually comes to me.

Sometimes, Joe wants to talk about an issue or problem in his life. Maybe his family. I'll listen for as long as he wants, because my role is to make his life easier. If we're doing the show in Los Angeles and he calls my hotel room at 2 A.M. to say his throat feels constricted and he needs to get to a hospital—which actually happened—I drive him.

Doing such things might seem to contradict the glamorous notion that I have all this power to shape the show and the talent. But Mika and Joe are the show. I do what has to be done to help them make *Morning Joe* as good as possible.

Our relationship does not work in reverse. I'm expected to work as hard as I can without burdening them with how my son is misbehaving or with complaints about the superintendent of my apartment building or with doubts about how much they respect me. They are on television for three hours every day. I'm not. I cannot make my personal life one more thing they must deal with.

So when Joe and Mika strode into C2B late in the morning of April 28, the first thing I did was apologize. Not for being sick. I know that's not something to apologize for. Instead, I was commiserating with them because their already crowded schedule now had to make room for the serious illness of a member of their team.

To Joe, I looked frightened. To Mika, I looked embarrassed at being the center of attention. I apparently looked like I could use comforting, too, because comfort is what Mika began to dispense. You don't look different, she said. You don't look like you've lost your mind. You are still with us here in the present, conscious, alert. You're fine.

She didn't know that. None of us did. She actually feared I might wind up damaged.

Louis, who had never left my side, was trying to keep up my spirits, too. In fact, he told me so many times that I was going to be okay I finally had to say, "Dude, I love you, but I need to hear that from a doctor."

Joe said little. He looked very grim. He said later he

could not be false by patting my shoulder and saying all would be well, because he thought my odds of getting out of this intact were miserable, no better than fifty-fifty.

Now Mika went into full Mika-mode.

She was all over her cell phone, calling the hospital CEO, calling hospital public relations officials, calling Jenny, calling Mom and Dad, reaching out to anyone who might help in the saving of me. She never stopped dialing.

Mika and Joe were swirling like superheroes who had arrived to confront the arch-villain in my head and to beat him senseless. They were becoming *my* executive producers. Just as I did for them and the show every morning, they had put on headsets of a sort and were working to make me come out right.

Mika pointed at her chest, then her butt.

"Mommy," she said, "is kicking ass."

My head was still pounding. I had no idea whether my brain was still bleeding. My wife was still a couple of hundred miles away. But this, this flattening of doors and taking of names, was starting to sink deeply into my heart.

So this is how much they care.

I could tell this wasn't Joe simply reverting to Congressman Scarborough. He wasn't making an obligatory stop to give a hospitalized constituent his best wishes for a full recovery and, after a two-minute visit, moving on to a ribbon cutting at a Pensacola strip mall. He was in this fight. He cared far more than I had assumed.

In the days ahead, as I lay in my hospital bed, I would get short e-mails from him that said nothing more than *Call me if you get bored* or *We miss you very much.* They were good enough to keep, and I have.

During these first hours I wasn't worried about Jenny, Andrew, or the future. There were no ruminations about how and why this event had happened. That would come later. By swooping in and taking charge, Mika and Joe had freed me to focus on the present task, which was fixing the problem. How do we do that? How do I get out of this? Who do we call, what doctor do I need? It was as self-centered as I had ever been.

Mika and Joe were aware that until now I had been the beneficiary of good fortune all my life. Not enough emotional pain had been inflicted, they sensed, to bequeath perspective and serenity as I went about my job. I was too young and too lucky to carry scars. Now change was coming. A transformation had begun in the backseat of the Escalade, and accelerated in C2B. A driven, focused, charmed man had been knocked to the floor by something no one saw coming.

"Usually, bad experiences, if you can survive them, are the best things that can happen to you," Mika says.

If you can survive them.

Joe, at my bedside, had an idea. He turned to Mika.

"Hey, do you have Joe's phone number on your cell?"

Joe Biden's, that is.

chapter seven

The Doctor

On the morning of my event, as we'll call it, Dr. Vivek Deshmukh, one of the most skilled neurosurgeons in the country, had yet to assume his current top medical post in Portland, Oregon. That wouldn't happen for four months. So as I lay on my bed in C2B, Dr. Deshmukh was across the street in a clinic affiliated with George Washington, in a closed consultation room where he was seeing a patient. An assistant interrupted to announce a phone call. She was insistent. Dr. Deshmukh excused himself and stepped out to one of the clinic's workstations.

"Hello, Doctor. Vice President Biden would like to speak to you."

He had never met Biden. He had never spoken with him. He did recognize Biden's voice, however, and was understandably amazed to find himself chatting with the second most powerful man on the planet on an otherwise mundane Wednesday.

"I know you're real busy," the vice president began. "I don't want to take up too much of your time because, unlike me, you're doing consequential things."

Dr. Deshmukh was impressed by the self-deprecating humor.

"I have a good friend in your ER," Biden went on, "and could you make time to see him? I've called around and asked many people who should be taking care of him, and everyone I've talked to has said you're the best doctor to take care of it."

The friend had bleeding in his brain, Biden said. He gave my name.

Not only did Dr. Deshmukh not know Biden personally, I didn't know Biden personally. He was not my friend, though I'd like to think he is now. Mika and Joe, however, knew him well. More relevant, they knew he was an aneurysm survivor.

Twenty-two years earlier, when he was forty-five, Biden had suffered not one but two aneurysms that had to be corrected with surgery, which somehow the politician in Joe Scarborough had remembered as he stood at my bedside in the emergency room. After describing my problem to one of Biden's aides, Mika had been put through instantly and, fighting through tears, had asked for help.

Biden did not hesitate. He would find the right guy.

The guy turned out to be Vivek Deshmukh, who had finished second in a class of 120 at the University of Florida College of Medicine and done his neurosurgical training at the Barrow Neurological Institute in Arizona, one of the world's best. That morning, he was director of cerebrovascular and endovascular neurosurgery at George Washington. As I would come to know, he is unflappable and skilled at reducing complexity to easily understood terms in a soft, reassuring voice.

Dr. Deshmukh told Biden he would, of course, help and, after hanging up, turned to the hospital's computer system to find my CAT scan.

It was ugly. He had seen a thousand like it. But it was ugly. There was a lot of blood loose in my head.

A brain has three linings, and my renegade blood was between the middle and the inner, the space where the brain's arteries and veins live. The middle lining is the arachnoid, because it looks like a spider's web, and any bleeding beneath it is thus a "subarachnoid hemorrhage."

The most common reason for blood to be loose there is blunt-force trauma, the sort of thing that happens in a traffic accident. That wasn't my problem, obviously. Another common reason is a rupture in an abnormal collection of blood vessels some people are born with. Dr. Deshmukh had in mind something else, the same thing I had raised with Dr. Mayersak. An aneurysm.

Cerebral aneurysms are balloonlike bulges in the walls of arteries, which are the high-pressure freeways that deliver blood from the heart throughout the body, as opposed to veins, which return blood to the heart at lower pressure. Where arteries fork, there's turbulence in the blood, which can lead to weakness in arterial walls, which can lead to the ballooning. An aneurysm can be as small as an eighth of an inch, as big as an inch and a quarter.

Statistics vary, but several million people have an aneurysm at this moment and do not know it. Most will probably live on in blissful ignorance, because their aneurysm will not cause symptoms or burst.

But each year in the United States, something like twenty-seven thousand aneurysms do rupture. That's seventy-four a day, three an hour. From looking at my CAT scan, Dr. Deshmukh was pretty certain that today had been Licht rupture day, which, if true, meant my life had moved closer to the abyss's edge.

If an aneurysm ruptures, there's no room for the blood

that escapes. The skull is not an expandable place. Pressure builds. The blood can irritate tissue. Other arteries can spasm and constrict, blocking themselves, which can lead to a stroke. Tissue can get squeezed against bone. The whole brain might shift. It's a potential cascade of malfunction.

About 15 percent of those whose aneurysms burst die before reaching a hospital. About 25 percent more die later. Of those who survive, most are permanently disabled by the invasion of blood into places it should not go. In the end, only about a fifth of those Americans whose aneurysms rupture live through the experience undamaged.

None of this did I know. It would be days before I did, not until I got home and surfed the Web and talked with Dad.

Examining my scan, Dr. Deshmukh could not tell how much damage had been done, because no scan can pick up the physical side effects of an aneurysm, like immobility or scrambled speech or blurred vision. He needed to see me in person to get a sense of those things, and he also needed a more detailed look at my brain. He called the neurologist on duty in the emergency room and ordered up a second CAT scan.

After finishing with his patient in the consultation

room at the clinic, he scampered across Twenty-third Street to the main building, into the ER, and down to the CAT suite. The second test would be done with contrasting dyes, the better to see my arteries. I had been delivered there before he arrived. It was sometime around noon.

I have no memory of this moment. I apparently have erased it just as I did Dr. Mayersak's first visit to me. As I lay on a table that would slide inside the CAT machine, Dr. Deshmukh asked me to describe what had happened and how I felt now. He asked if I had any allergies, surgeries, or medical problems.

Now came another variation of the already familiar neurological quiz.

What is your name?

Where are you?

Do you know what year it is?

I knew the answers, knew them all, and that was good at least. Except for the head pain and the initial scan that showed considerable bleeding, the doctor concluded I was an otherwise healthy young man who was aware he was in trouble, but not catatonic or fidgeting or wailing with grief. Stoic, he thought.

Into the machine I went. Into my arm through an IV went the contrast solution. The hunt for my aneurysm was on. The CAT machine began methodically imaging my head in slices 2.5mm wide. Dr. Deshmukh examined the images, one after another.

Nothing. No aneurysm.

Yet there was so much blood. That much almost always means an aneurysm.

Where is it?

A doctor wants to get inside and repair the artery. But he has to find the scene of the microscopic disaster first. Dr. Deshmukh feared he was missing something. If he sent a patient home without finding the aneurysm, it could rupture again, perhaps fatally. Mine should be easy to find, yet there was no evidence of it.

The doctor wanted the next level of test, the gold standard, a cerebral angiogram, a test that makes possible a much higher degree of magnification of the arteries. We were entering a phase of the afternoon I do remember.

I was taken upstairs to the "angio suite," a chilly, sterile room with multiple monitors and a machine that seemed as big as a Buick. As I was wheeled in, there were people milling about. One pointed down at me on the hospital bed and mouthed to the others a single word, "Biden."

Joe and Mika had told me they were reaching out to the vice president. Now I was seeing the results. Now I was becoming a celebrity, which wasn't all that unusual for a hospital in the same neighborhood as the White House, the Capitol, the Supreme Court, the embassies of dozens of nations, and most cabinet-level departments of the government.

I had no problem with the special attention. When your head feels as if someone has put a belt around it and yanked with both hands, when they've told you that you might have an aneurysm, when your emotions have careened into unexplored lands, you want special attention. You want somebody to make a call if that somebody knows somebody.

The hospital, in any event, probably would have reacted to my case in precisely the same way even if Biden had never gotten involved. In the emergency room, Dr. Mayersak hadn't known he would be, yet she had sounded the neurological claxon as soon as she had the proof. Dr. Deshmukh might have been summoned anyway.

In the angio suite, they seemed to be in a good mood, which helped me. The anesthesiologist announced she would be my cocktail waitress. The guy who was going to shave my right leg as part of the procedure noted he was providing a bikini waxing. I was counting on this test. I wanted to be told the bleeding had stopped. I didn't know anything about aneurysms, but I assumed unchecked bleeding could not be good.

My leak almost certainly had stopped already, though, which Dr. Deshmukh now told me. Ruptures tend to be quick affairs. The aneurysm seals itself. But that might not last. A re-rupture at any time is possible. That's why it was important to find the spot.

A consent form was put in front of me. I hesitated.

During a cerebral angiogram, an incision is made in the patient's leg, and a small-diameter catheter is inserted into the femoral artery. Using arteries, it then travels up through the torso and into the neck. Dye is shot through the catheter, erupting at the other end like a fountain, providing excellent contrast in the brain for that big Buick of a machine to snap images.

But to the body, the catheter is an alien disrupter that needs to be attacked. Blood can coagulate on it, and a clot can break away, travel, and stop, blocking an artery and causing a stroke. There is, in other words, a risk to a cerebral angiogram. Not much of one, but a risk.

I did not pause in signing the consent form because I'm a guy who loves control. That trait only involves the control room. It doesn't extend to reading the fine print on every single document. I paused only because I had come so very far so very fast. I had been doing a show and now I was in a strange room with all these people and the vice president was involved and my brain had blood and nothing was right.

But I knew there was no choice. Small, theoretical risk from a catheter vs. devastating, actual pain in my brain from an unknown cause?

Dr. Deshmukh nudged me along.

"Mr. Licht," he said, "you're very, very sick. You need to get this done *now*. Sign the form."

I signed the form.

My doctor had done more than two thousand cerebral angiograms. As daring and complicated as it sounds to thread a tube such a long way through a body, from leg to head, he made the journey to the base of my skull in no more than ninety seconds, using a live monitor to watch the catheter's travels. I could feel it as it went, a very odd sensation, but they had given me some excellent drugs so I wouldn't squirm at the thought of being threaded like a human needle. The drugs didn't put me out, because they weren't intended to. Dr. Deshmukh needed me awake to follow his instructions.

"Take a deep breath in, hold your breath, don't breathe or move," he began.

A shot of dye raced through the catheter, into my head. A feeling of warm, suffusing liquid ensued. I wouldn't recommend it.

"Breathe," the doctor said.

We did this sequence of hold-your-breath, shoot-the-dye, release-your-breath twenty times or so. Sometimes the dye caused little sparkly lightning bolts in my eyes. For an hour, the machine rotated through all kinds of angles, snapping images that Dr. Deshmukh and the angio team could see on monitors.

"You find anything yet?" I said.

"So far, it's looking okay."

He meant that, other than the blood, everything looked normal, which was both good and complicating. Good because there was no aneurysm, complicating because there was no aneurysm. If there is one to be found, the very first cerebral angiogram almost always finds it. Not this time. The doctor peered more closely at the images to make sure he wasn't missing something. He wasn't. He was so certain he would see an aneurysm. He was troubled.

What is the source of this blood?

When we finished, they wheeled me upstairs to the intensive care unit, which would be my home as they watched for signs of secondary damage and until they could do more exploration to find out what was going on inside my head. Passing a sign in the ICU that said NO BARE HANDS, I was rolled into Room 284, which had a single bed and a wall that was nothing but windows, looking out on the low-rise skyline of Washington.

Not long after, Jenny walked in.

chapter eight

Jenny

In the early years, Jenny Blanco came to a couple of unequivocal conclusions about me.

"This guy's a real jerk."

"I hate him."

Our relationship began telephonically around 1998, and it was only professional, journalist to journalist. She was the producer of the 11 P.M. news at NBC in San Diego, I was the producer of the 11 P.M. news at NBC in Los Angeles, and sometimes Jenny would call and ask for help covering a breaking story on my turf. Those were reasonable requests, given that our stations were siblings and her show did not have the resources mine did. We had a helicopter. We had four camera crews. We had three reporters.

NBC's late news in Los Angeles had the biggest audience west of the Mississippi River then, and there I was at its helm, mid-twenties, not long removed from college and even less long removed from my serendipitous start in television as a writer on the O.J. show. As a result, I could be insufferably arrogant. Jenny Blanco? She was that producer on the phone from a much smaller station who made annoying requests of the very busy me. It's difficult to believe, but somehow she wound up feeling second class.

Then, one day, Jenny came up to L.A. to go to a party I had been invited to as well. At last, like two fated lovers in a fable, the telephone voices came face-to-face for the first time, and Jenny left with a distinct, fresh impression of Mr. Licht.

"He's an overgrown frat boy."

She couldn't believe this creature had seemed intimidating. He was a kid. "I still hated him." In time, she left Southern California for San Francisco and then a job with MSNBC in New York, not saying good-bye because there was no reason to, because she possessed nothing but antipathy for me. She might have possessed even more antipathy if she had known I had told my station's executives not to hire her if she ever applied for a job. To be honest, I feared the competition; I could tell she was smart and good.

Years later, years without contact between us, I went to 30 Rock to see network executives, and while strolling through the newsroom of NBC's local station I came across Jenny, by now producer of the 11 P.M. news in the nation's biggest market. Wow, I thought, she looks great. We chatted. She immediately wondered if I was being sweet simply because she had attained market acceptability.

She was correct.

Sir Romance.

But professional success is, indeed, an attractive quality, and one of the things most attractive about Jenny to this day is that she's successful and driven.

Now began the longest pursuit of my dating days, longest in time and longest in distance. I was living in the Bay Area because NBC had bought a station in San Jose and asked me to move from Los Angeles to help oversee its integration into the NBC way of doing things. This meant many trips to New York to talk with management.

With another coming, I e-mailed Jenny to tell her about a job that was open at our station. Perhaps you'd be interested, I noted. Perhaps we should talk. Perhaps we should have a drink. She read this for what it was, a backdoor request for a date, a "total scam," but she did consent to meet at an Irish pub in Manhattan one night after her 11 P.M. show had ended. She arrived with a "let's get this over with" air and no makeup. More than three hours later, she says, she left with a "he's not so bad" feeling. The years had sandpapered a bit of my cockiness.

Though separated by the entire United States of America, we managed to go out a few times, and while I thought Jenny liked me, she regarded each get-together as nothing more than collegial. "We can hang out," she said, "but it's not going to go any further than that." Her argument was we worked for the same company and had similar jobs and those were ingredients that should never be combined with a personal relationship, period.

I tried to talk her out of this. Why, I said, do women always think ahead to the worst case? We are not about to get married. It's dating, not betrothal. Why not see what happens? If something does, we'll figure out what to do.

One night, on a rooftop deck of a friend's apartment in New York, I expounded like this for forty-five minutes, trying to break her resistance and winding up nowhere. Ever since I was a teen, I have known what my wife would be like, someone smart, beautiful, warm, independent, and successful. And dark-haired, which Jenny is. Nobody before had met every item on my list. She did. I wasn't ready to declare her The One, but neither was I ready to give up merely because of a hurdle like being in the NBC family together.

In the end, oddly, it was precisely because we worked

for the same company that the walls came down. Both of us were dispatched to Athens in the summer of 2004 as part of NBC's coverage of the Olympics, and out of the shared pressure, fatigue, frustration, and exhilaration of covering a monumental event emerged a seriously hooked couple. A few weeks later, I brought Jenny to my sister Stephanie's wedding. I saw how easily and warmly she blended with my family. (My family was always my strongest dating asset because Mom and Dad have been together since high school, suggesting long commitment runs in the genes.) And Dad was completely smitten with my date.

In most relationships, the sides begin as exemplars of polite, reasonable behavior and only later do the shields drop and the irritating flaws materialize. But Jenny and I never went through the poseur phase. Our relationship started badly; she disliked me long before she liked. And at the Olympics, I had seen every Jenny there was. Tired Jenny. Crying Jenny. Tough Jenny. Neither of us was going to be surprised by the other because we already knew each other so well.

Months of bicoastal dating unfolded. We never went more than two without seeing each other. Once, when Jenny was sick in New York and I was in San Francisco, I called ten restaurants in Manhattan trying to find one that would deliver chicken soup to her apartment as a surprise. (I found one; they added a brownie, too.)

Jenny was the first person who made me think of someone other than myself. Before she came into my life, I was only about me and my work. All you had to do was check out my wardrobe. I had NBC hats, NBC T-shirts, NBC jackets, NBC backpacks. And I wore that stuff constantly. But Jenny quickly came to mean so much to me that I pledged I would never do anything to mess up the relationship I had finally convinced her to have. "I'll never break up with you," I told her. "It will never come from me."

Every decision I made was geared to keeping her and making sure she kept me. Jenny will tell you that from the moment we reconnected years after California, I was a model of thoughtfulness, which folks at 30 Rock will consider headline news. One time, before we became a serious couple, I was invited to an out-of-town wedding and asked Jenny if she would like to join me. When she said yes, I made sure our hotel room had two beds. With anybody else, I would not have thought of being as gentlemanly. Even killer producers can be softened.

Our two-city relationship could never work for long, of course, because there were too many sad airport farewells. The only choice was to do something I had never done,

which was put the personal ahead of the professional by moving to New York. I did not care what job I landed as long as it was with NBC and I was with Jenny.

Having been at big local news stations, I assumed my résumé would induce salivation in New York, but nobody at the network seemed impressed, nor did anyone at the local station, WNBC. So one day, I sat down with an executive for the little-sister cable network, MSNBC, which at that time was based not at 30 Rock but in Secaucus, just across the Hudson River.

The MSNBC executive had no job either. Maybe later. I was being escorted out of his office when I blurted out that I'd like to talk with Phil Griffin, who was then the cable network's vice president of prime time. We had known each other at the *Today* show, where he was a producer and I a college intern, so Phil agreed to talk to the supplicant. But he only half listened. I was getting nowhere. He launched into an autopilot seminar about how cable news is more opinionated than broadcast. I didn't mention that I found cable news unwatchable. Finally, Phil asked why I was moving back east.

"I'm dating Jenny Blanco," I said.

"You're dating Jenny Blanco! Oh my God! I love her. I hated that she left!"

Jenny, remember, had worked for MSNBC before switching to the New York local station. Phil regarded her as a smart, serious, levelheaded goddess. If she was dating me, I must be a superior being. "I trust her judgment any day," Phil says now. Immediately his enthusiasm for my application rose, doors opened, and before long I had an offer to be a senior producer of an MSNBC show called *Scarborough Country*. I had never seen it. I had no idea who Joe Scarborough was.

It was difficult, taking this new job. The only news I had ever done was broadcast and local, and I was a big deal in that familiar world. I was nothing in cable news and my new job was a lesser one, compared to what I had done. But it would be in New York, hub of all things media. And the move wasn't about me, it was about us, Jenny and me, and I had promised to do whatever it took to preserve us.

A week after arriving to start with *Scarborough Country*, I proposed to her during a previously planned trip to Acapulco. A year later, at a hotel overlooking the Pacific Ocean just north of San Diego, where Jenny had grown up, 150 people watched our marriage begin.

At the rehearsal dinner the night before, my sister made a speech she had carefully typed. Stephanie began by saying that most of her life, her older brother could be

pretty focused on himself, demanding, driven, sharing few feelings, willing to be unpopular to get what he wanted. Then, she said, I met Jenny. Remember that scene in *Jerry Maguire* where Tom Cruise tells Renée Zellweger, "You complete me"? Well, that's what Stephanie said Jenny does for me.

She's even made me a better dresser. I'm not nearly the sartorial commercial for NBC I used to be. My relationship with her kind of sums me up. You might not like me when we first meet, but you'll warm up after a while. If I hadn't met her, if we hadn't clicked, I don't know how I would have gotten through what was happening to me in George Washington Hospital.

chapter nine

A Jacket

As Jenny entered my ICU room, the only thing I could blurt out, for the second time that day, was an observation of magnificent dumbness. It came nowhere close to conveying my joy.

"You're here," I said. "You came."

Jenny had spent the previous few moments in a bathroom outside my room, lecturing herself about how important it was not to add to my fears by dissolving in front of me. Jenny is a crier. But the woman who now came to my bed was neither distraught nor frightened as she took my hand, but radiant and calm.

"I love you," she said.

To her I looked, considering the brain bleed, not too bad. This was an odd thing about my event. I never *looked* sick. I was probably the least sick-looking patient in the

ICU. No bruises, cuts, punctures, rashes, spots. No limbs in casts. I wasn't weak. My breathing was fine and my heart chugging along. The malfunction was out of sight, visible only with exquisitely calibrated technology, and manifesting itself, so far, only as a horrible headache.

Before entering, Jenny had imagined her husband might be unconscious or unable to talk. She could tell by my eyes, though, I was still operating in the here and now. We said very little to each other, because the usual first questions between spouses already had answers. How was your day? A personal worst. And yours? Same.

Ever since Louis reached her as she was feeding Andrew in his high chair that morning, she had been in motion from our apartment on the Upper West Side of Manhattan to Penn Station in Midtown and then down the East Coast via Amtrak. She had been in perpetual communication with my parents, Mika, my sister, her father, and our babysitter, who took control of Andrew as Jenny departed.

She hadn't tried to call me. If I was in the hospital, where I had never been, I was too bad off to disturb. Someone had said "aneurysm" to her in the flurry of calls, and brain bleeding, but Jenny had no more knowledge of the medical technicalities and risks than I or any layman did.

But she knew it must be bad, because she knew my parents were now bound for Washington and "they are not dramatic or overreactors."

On the train, Jenny did not fast-forward to a world in which I had died. Get there. That was all. Work the problem. Because she had no idea what she would find at the other end, her three or four hours of travel were beyond anxious, even weird. As the train passed through New Jersey and Philadelphia and into Maryland, folks at CNN's *Anderson Cooper 360* reached her. She had been working for CNN part-time but had been discussing a full-time job with them. Now, on this day of all days, they offered it, having no clue where she was going or why. She was apologetic. Could this be discussed later?

Louis reached Phil Griffin at 30 Rock, where he is now president of MSNBC. Phil went online to search "aneurysm" and the more he read, the worse he felt. He knew how much I loved being at the center of *Morning Joe*. It seemed quite possible that some sort of disability would end my career.

My sister, Stephanie, reached Marc Nespoli. My best friend—I was the best man at his wedding, he at mine— grew up to be a psychiatrist, and after he heard from Stephanie, his thoughts reverted to something that had happened during his medical training at a Vermont hospital. One of his patients, a nineteen-year-old man who was being treated for seizures, suddenly summoned nurses to his room in the middle of the night because he had "the worst headache" of his life. He died of a subarachnoid hemorrhage a short time later. In other words, unlike me, Marc knew firsthand the threat posed by a ruptured aneurysm. He, too, felt a need to get to Washington quickly.

Mike Barnicle, who had been with us on *Morning Joe* that morning, was at his hotel when he was called. Mike marvels at the intensity gap between newspapers, where he grew up professionally, and television, where he now lives. At his old paper, the *Boston Globe*, you wrote a story or column for the next day, which was stressful for a few hours, but there was no prompt verdict on the quality of your words. Circulation data didn't arrive the next day, and even when it did, it did not offer a measurement of the worth of your story specifically, only the paper's value as a whole.

At *MJ*, new ratings arrive every afternoon on my BlackBerry and up and down the corridors of 30 Rock, measuring the popularity not merely of the show, but of each eight- or ten-minute segment. Who watched at that moment? How long did they watch? Happiness or failure,

Mike says, "comes right down the hallway, like an ocean wave." He wonders how any of us handle it. Among his first thoughts now was that my brain had shorted out from the crazy intensity of network television.

It was my parents who had known about my emergency the longest, because I had called them first after my brain popped. After my call, my father the doctor and my mother the physician's associate had gone about their day in Connecticut, not terribly worried because there was no evidence yet they should be. But then Jenny telephoned, then Mika, then Joe, and with each call things got worse. Dad and Mom decided they had to get to my bedside. Then, as they prepared to go, Joe called again.

"I just spoke with the neurosurgeon, Dr. Deshmukh," Joe said, "and he says the situation is very serious and you should come down immediately."

Dad couldn't believe the phrasing Joe had used. Was he saying what it sounded like?

To Dad, you would never tell a relative on the phone that a loved one is dying. What if that relative was at the wheel of a car at that moment? What if she was in the kitchen, fainted, and hit her head on the counter?

No, you would euphemize until you could tell the relative face-to-face and provide comfort and assistance. You would keep it vague on the phone, not saying death was imminent, but saying only that things were serious. As Joe just had.

Was he deliberately resorting to this sort of compassionate haze to avoid saying I was dying? Or had he inadvertently chosen a wording not realizing how a doctor might interpret it? For a moment—perhaps the worst of his life, he said later—Dad saw a void opening beneath his feet. He might not be able to handle what seemed to be happening, the death of his son.

"Hold it," he said to Joe. "You have just seen Chris. Is there any difference whatsoever in how he is from the time he went into the hospital to the time you last saw him?"

Joe would have to be specific now. Either I could still talk coherently, as I could when I had called Dad a few hours before and he had sent me to the hospital, or I could not, because the aneurysm had begun to wreck my brain, which would mean we were headed for something catastrophic.

"Oh, yeah, he's fine," Joe said.

He did not mean fine as in healthy. He meant nothing had changed since my symptoms had first erupted. I was stable. Dad saw the void close. But he knew the situation remained grave, even if it was not deteriorating. I might be headed for brain surgery. The doctor in him knew too much about the risk of opening a skull and venturing inside with instruments. Surgery might repair the aneurysm, but collateral damage was always possible. Would I have all my functions when I left the operating room?

At least for now, I was neurologically all right and safely in a hospital, a big one, full of neurosurgeons who could react if my brain seemed to worsen. "It's sort of like in a poker game," Dad says, "and everything you own is on the table. That's the bad news. The good news is, you have a pretty good hand."

Looking back, being a pile of chips is sort of how I felt.

Now Dad, a man who deals in facts and eschews drama, did something uncharacteristic, practically superstitious. As he and Mom frantically packed to make the train that would take them to Washington, he became obsessed with finding a certain lightweight, outdoor jacket of his. It had been a gift from me, brought from the Vancouver Olympics two months earlier. He had worn it to work that morning and now felt he had to take it with him. It was a link to his son, who was in danger.

He couldn't find it. He looked everywhere. He and

Mom even drove back to their medical office to look. Not there either. They had to leave without it.

Except they didn't, because the jacket was in Dad's suitcase, where he himself had put it, an act that stress and uncertainty had promptly obliterated from his memory.

chapter ten

A Kiss

I was an exhausted lab rat as evening came.

Poked and drugged, scanned by huge machines. A catheter had taken a cruise through my torso, my brain had been squirted with dyes, and I hadn't eaten since before dawn, when I got up to do MJ.

The hospital brought food of some sort, maybe soup and crackers, and I know I drank a lot of ginger ale, but nothing could overcome the sensation of having gone a thousand rounds with a battalion of heavyweights. The head pounding had entered its ninth hour. The emotional tank was on empty.

Yet I didn't feel I could give in to fatigue. My brain couldn't be trusted, which was a sorry thing to say about it after we had spent so many happy years together. If I shut it down for sleep, it might not restart. No one had said that; I just believed it.

I don't remember which doctor it was, but in the past few hours one had tried to buck me up by saying a good percentage of folks with a ruptured aneurysm—if that's what I had—go on to lead pretty normal lives.

A good percentage? That's it? "Good" sounded like "not too many."

My spirit did not soar.

For the first time, including Andrew's birth, thoughts of work were not racing through my head. I didn't care about it, which was liberating, but there wasn't much choice. My brain could not handle anything other than its own dysfunction. There was no room to ponder what guests had been booked for tomorrow or what hot topics we might pursue. Mentally, I had to surrender as executive producer of *Morning Joe*.

Besides, Mika and Joe at some point had said they would not be doing *MJ* tomorrow. They'd leave the hosting duties to Willie Geist because they were too upset. At the time, I really didn't believe they would skip it. But they did. In retrospect, this became part of my education. Wow, they didn't do a show because of me? They were that concerned? The file of evidence that perhaps I worried too much was thickening.

At 5:45 P.M. on that first day, Dr. Deshmukh entered my ICU room, adding to the standing-room-only gathering. Joe, Mika, Louis, Jenny, me. The doctor was going to give a status report, and Jenny remembers he exuded calm competence. As he spoke, the reporter in Mika scribbled on the backs of two sheets of paper apparently provided by Louis, because one was a printout of one of his e-mails and the other was a copy of Joe and Mika's schedule for that day. She gave me those notes as a souvenir.

Exactly twelve hours earlier, at 5:45 A.M., we had been fifteen minutes from airtime. Who knew when I'd get to do another show.

Dr. Deshmukh began by saying the arteries within my brain looked fine. None of the scans—and I'd had three by now—had found the characteristic signs of an aneurysm.

"That," he said, "doesn't make me feel any better."

There was no doubt I had a subarachnoid hemorrhage. And the blood had to have come from somewhere. It wasn't fiction.

"I am still very nervous about you," he said. "I am concerned you have an aneurysm that's not detected. In a week, it may show up. If and when we find it, we go in and get it."

Sometimes, it can even take three cerebral angiograms to locate the weak point in the arterial system. Clearly, I would be at George Washington for a while. If nothing were found during a second angio, Dr. Deshmukh said, maybe I could go home in two weeks.

Two weeks.

Lots of patients are hospitalized for their ailments far longer, but two weeks seemed an eternity to someone who had never been in a hospital. My headaches would last even longer, Dr. Deshmukh said, until the runaway blood was absorbed back into my system.

He did not go into detail about what "go in and get it" meant, but there are two common ways. One involves an interior journey very much like the cerebral angiogram. A catheter is pushed through the patient's arteries, this time all the way to the scene of the crime. A coil of wire—thinner than a strand of hair—is pushed through the catheter and jammed into the balloon of the aneurysm. That fills it and seals it off from the artery, eliminating the weak spot through which blood has escaped.

Sometimes, though, the balloon is so tiny no coil can fit inside. Or sometimes its neck is so wide any coil shoved

inside will fall back out, dropping into the main blood-stream, where it could lead to a stroke. In those cases, the second type of fix is used: brain surgery.

Dr. Deshmukh felt I was a candidate for number two, but he kept that to himself. He hadn't found an aneurysm, which probably meant mine was really, really small and coiling would probably not be possible. Instead, when he found the microscopic assailant, he would go in through the skull and pinch off the aneurysm with a titanium clip. It's not as awful or dangerous as it sounds, he says. Surgery is more invasive than going the interior route, yes, but getting rid of aneurysms this way has been done for half a century.

If I had known brain surgery was in my future, however, I wouldn't have felt better that it had been done for half a century.

Dr. Deshmukh could not close off the aneurysm by either means, of course, if he could not find it. For now, he was calling a halt to the hunt. He does not like to do cerebral angiograms one after another in a constant quest for the aneurysm. For one thing, the procedure itself has risk. And in the immediate aftermath of a rupture, the body can camouflage the scene, and it can take several days for things to settle and the aneurysm become easier to see. Be-

cause he hadn't seen mine after the first angio, there was a chance it was being obscured in just this way. It made little sense to search again so soon. He would do a second cerebral angiogram a week from today.

Until then, we had to be alert for any neurological sign that the aneurysm, wherever it was, was rupturing a second time. The odds of that were not great and they diminished each day, but the threat was real. He did not say this either, but Dr. Deshmukh has had patients who survive the initial rupture, are safely ensconced in the intensive care unit, and then suffer new bleeding and die before they can get to surgery.

In other words, patients who were in precisely my situation.

My ignorance was my happiness.

But maybe it wasn't an aneurysm, the doctor went on. In about 15 percent of cases, no definitive reason for the bleeding is found. It's a mysterious one-off event, unlikely to happen again. But he still had an obligation to keep hunting.

Even if there was no aneurysm and I never re-bled, there was one last serious matter.

The blood already there.

Until it was absorbed, it was an irritant. I heard that

a lot. An irritant. Apparently, the renegade blood could irritate me into a stroke by causing my healthy arteries to spasm, and the most likely time frame for that was between five and ten days from now. I was to start taking a pill every two hours, nimodipine, whose purpose was to prevent arterial spasms.

Dr. Deshmukh recalls that at some point during his briefing, I asked whether I would be able to go back to work. "This is a guy who's accustomed to go, go, go, four in the morning to whatever late hours in the day," he says. I didn't seem concerned I might never be able to do my job again, he says. It was more that my schedule had blown up. He knows the type. "They want to go back to work right away, and they don't like being in the hospital and they don't like taking time off."

No, we don't.

So that's where things stood. Possible re-bleeds? Possible spasms? I was in more precarious shape than I had thought.

And the day wasn't done.

Though I finally felt ready to succumb to sleep, I had to endure one more test.

Sometimes, the culprit in cases like mine is a tumor in the brain or on the spinal cord that ruptures and releases blood, mimicking the symptoms of a ruptured aneurysm. Dr. Deshmukh didn't think that's what had happened to me, but he wanted to rule it out. The test is a long one involving an MRI, and most patients hate it.

I hated it.

They held off this test until Mom and Dad arrived, well into the night now, coming directly from the train station, where they had been picked up by an NBC car. Willie Geist, who had not been with us on the trip to Washington, had come from New York on the same train, and remembers thinking as he walked in how vulnerable I looked, hooked to monitors, pale, whipped. It was so not me, he thought.

Agreed.

I thought I saw tears in Mom's eyes. Dad, knowing how much I like to control things, knew that being in this whole mess would drive me crazy. He was about to be so right.

I was wheeled away to another suite, put on another hard-surface slab, and once again slid into a machine. This one clicked relentlessly, loudly. I was not medicated this time because the test was not invasive. I was much more aware than during the cerebral angiogram.

As I lay there for twenty minutes, thirty, listening to

the clicking, silently objecting to my lack of command over anything in my life right now, the whole day rose up and punched me. There was no good to any of this. Everything sucked. The brain bleed, the tests, the fatigue, the disruption, the inability to find the thing in my head. All sucked. Why I thought there should be some good in all this, I don't know, but I found none. The thoughts were precursors of much bigger, darker ones that would descend upon me in a week. I lay there silently in the MRI machine with nothing to do but indulge my irritation.

Why does the slab have to be so hard? Who fucking designed this thing to be that hard? We can put someone on the moon and this machine has to be so loud I can't even hear myself think? And, honestly, how long does it take to do a map of my brain?

Then I was silent no longer.

"Enough!" I yelled. "Done!"

When I got back from the MRI, Mom and Dad and Jenny were still in my room. It was late now. My parents would spend the night at a hotel NBC had found for them and would pay for. Jenny would have to leave soon, too; hospital rules. As my parents began to go, Dad stopped and returned to my bed. He bent close to my ear, and whispered.

"I absolutely fucking guarantee you that you will be all right," he said.

He didn't know if I had heard this, because I seemed so tired and beaten up. But I remember his vow now. It gave me hope. Dad never lies. Dad never coddles. If he was promising I was going to be all right, then I was going to be all right.

He leaned close and kissed me.

$$\left[\,\textit{chapter eleven}\,\right]$$

The Caller

Though I long ago gave up, quite willingly, the ambition of being an anchor or reporter, I was often on the air during a typical *MJ*. In Control Room 3A at 30 Rock, there's always a small camera focused on my chair in the front row because I sometimes banter with Joe and Mika during a show, usually about e-mails viewers have sent while we're live. They have become used to seeing the young executive producer in his dress shirt with no tie, sleeves rolled up, headset clamped over short, wavy hair.

My absence would be noticeable as time rolled on. And on the first day after my event, it would be really noticeable that Mika and Joe weren't there. So from NBC's famed Washington bureau, Willie Geist explained to those at home what was going on.

"Our friend Chris Licht was admitted to a Washington

hospital yesterday after experiencing extreme head pain," Willie said. "A subsequent CAT scan led doctors to believe Chris had suffered an aneurysm."

Since childhood, I have enjoyed the thrill and excitement of covering news, but never had I been the news being covered. My brain bleed was inverting the natural order.

"Chris is in stable condition," Willie went on, "and suffered no neurological effects from the incident. We expect him to make a full recovery. We do ask that you please keep Chris in your prayers."

I am not religious, and in the past my reaction upon hearing that someone was praying for someone else was entirely cynical. Good for you, terrific. Now people were going to pray for me. Jenny's aunt, a nun in Boston, even made sure my name was included among those for whom her congregation was to pray at Mass. All this felt rather good, surprisingly. I liked the idea that spiritual thoughts were traveling through the cosmos on my behalf. Whatever might work to get me out of this, I was in favor of.

I didn't see or hear Willie read his statement because the television in my ICU room offered many channels but MSNBC was not one of them, a source of frustration during my entire stay. Nor, therefore, did I see him chat on

the air a few minutes later with Mike Allen, the chief political writer of the Web site Politico, who had mentioned
my brain bleed in his column that day, a column read by
the same people who watch *MJ*, namely, the entire political universe.

But not long after all this discussion on the air, it became clear somebody must have said something about me,
because my BlackBerry lit up with e-mails. Jenny now had
possession of it as a precaution against my worst tenden-
cies, and she began reading aloud the things that were
flooding in. E-mails from people at NBC I hardly knew.
People at NBC I'd had disagreements with. Civilians who
were fans of the show, maybe had seen my face.

Thinking of you.

Get well.

It was merely the beginning. In time, Chris Matthews,
the host of *Hardball* on MSNBC, would send a note saying, *Aren't you the guy who created that morning show that's
got all the buzz? Let me know if you want my movie collection—or to come visit and love you close up.* Doris Wood of
Surprise, Arizona, said she really missed seeing me on the
air. Linda Tatum of Fort Riley, Kansas, said I needed to
hurry back because Joe, Mika, and Willie "need experience to balance them out (smile)." Bonnie McGregor of

Menlo Park, California, wanted the show to keep giving updates about my condition because I do such a good job with the production values, she said. And Brian Williams, the anchor of the *NBC Evening News*, sent a letter saying my event had sent a chill through 30 Rock because so many admired me.

This was overwhelming, especially the reaction from colleagues. I didn't know about all this admiration Brian mentioned. I assumed my fan base was limited. After all, a killer producer, as he goes about his killing, inflicts casualties. If the show matters above all else, as it did to me, hurting someone's feelings by being tough or brusque is an inevitable result.

I was aware enough of my reputation to have set out to be nicer and send fewer nasty e-mails, and I was making progress. But the affection and concern now floating into my hospital room electronically was a revelation, one that penetrated to my core. Any place has its feuds, and MSNBC can have ideological ones because some shows lean left and Joe Scarborough is more conservative. But the e-mails said, in effect, that nobody was focused on that. People were thinking of Chris the guy, the one in the hospital bed, not Chris the producer. I was so touched by this that in the aftermath of my illness, if I know you and

I find out you're sick, you'll get a note from me. Never did that before. Getting good wishes when you're in a tough spot means a lot. Trust me.

What happened next, however, was quite ridiculous.

I began to think I wasn't sick enough.

These notes are very nice. They reflect genuine concern. And yet, other than a really bad headache and intravenous tubes, I feel fine. I feel like me. Doctors have gone in and found nothing other than the blood. This could amount to nothing but a freak, minor thing. Am I really worthy of the attention in these e-mails? Am I going to seem like the boy who cried wolf? Will people feel burned if I turn out to be fine and they got all worked up for nothing?

At this point, remember, I didn't know the full risk I faced because I didn't know all the statistics, the ones suggesting that the number of people in my situation who emerge whole is only a very fortunate minority. If I had known that, I might not have been anxious about whether I warranted these e-mails and letters.

But I was anxious now.

Now came a complementary thought.

If all these people were sending all these e-mails, they must think I'm in terrible shape. They must think I'm a vegetable. If you announce, as Willie had, that someone is expected to make a full recovery, that's crap, isn't it? That's another way of saying that for now, as we speak, the poor guy is not doing too well at all.

In the corridors of the national media, which were the ones I cared about, they would assume I was done, no longer young, no longer energetic, no longer a killer. Although made with the best of intent, Willie's statement suggested that the master and commander of *Morning Joe* was now fragile.

I couldn't be seen that way. In my job, everybody looks to bully and take advantage. If you're a pushover, you get run over. And that's what people would think. As I lay there in the hospital, I might well have stopped caring about the particulars of the next *MJ*, but I still cared about my professional standing, even with a brain bleed. My education-through-illness wasn't far enough along yet for me to not care what people thought.

Three days later, on May 2, Mika and Joe did a special Sunday edition of the show from the lawn of the White House. We had long planned this, because the White House Correspondents' Association dinner was going to take place the night before and it would be fun to rehash the jokes and the celebrity sightings and President Obama's remarks.

That dinner is one of my favorites, and it was depressing to miss it, but Jenny and I had at least watched on C-SPAN. But without MSNBC available in my room, I couldn't see the special *MJ* the next morning. So we called NBC from my hospital room, and Jenny and I listened on speakerphone to a live feed of the show on a call-in line.

Someone told Joe I was parked there, eavesdropping.

He decided this caller had to be heard.

I hadn't prepared for this. But right away, I liked the idea. Joe seemed to sense I would be worried about my image. If he put me on the air, if only by phone, people out there would hear my voice, hear my thoughts, and realize I was still me. Even better, my health was improving already. They had done another CAT scan because my head really hurt, and it had shown the blood was being reabsorbed faster than expected.

Sitting in director's chairs with the White House behind them, Mika and Joe looked as if they had partied way too much at the dinner. They wore sunglasses. But they and Willie were chipper as they cued up the caller from the hospital. They began by noting that Alec Baldwin had asked about me at the dinner the previous night.

"How are you feeling right now, Chris," Joe said, "and how are they treating you at GW?"

For a nanosecond, I stammered slightly, then got going.

"I feel a lot better. Really turned the corner yesterday, and they couldn't be treating me any better, which is largely because Mika got on the phone and you got on the phone, and they've just been amazing here."

My voice was finding its stride.

"A lot of outpouring, which has really helped, and I will say I don't think the ICU has seen anything like you two last night before the dinner."

Mika and Joe had shown the television audience photos of themselves in their formalwear visiting my room, Mika draped across my bed and leaning in to give a kiss. My face was cherry with embarrassment.

"I know this will shock you, Chris," Joe said, "but since you've left we've missed every break."

"And last night, we had no idea where to go," Mika said, meaning I hadn't been there to steer them around the dinner. "We were lost."

They were keeping it light, which suggested all was fine with me and this was temporary.

"Well," I said, "if you want to know just how bored I am in the hospital, you ever wonder who looks at the online feed of the people at the dinner before the dinner actually starts? That was me."

"That is dark." Willie laughed.

"You were in a dark, dark place," Joe said.

I was keeping it light, too, because I could. See, brain working.

Mika, Joe, and I joked later that I really should have drooled and slurred as many words as possible, because that would come to be what people assumed I was like anyway.

chapter twelve

A Head in a Lap

In the midst of this, something else huge was under way in the life of the Lichts. A few days into my hospital stay—I can't remember when; the days blended—Jenny entered my room in the intensive care unit wearing a smile and waving an ultrasound photo that George Washington's radiology department had taken that morning.

The photo showed BLT, as we called it.

Baby Licht Two.

A blood test done before my event had revealed Jenny's new pregnancy, although we had told almost no one. She had been scheduled to have a confirming ultrasound in New York but had to skip it after my brain bleed. GW had been asking if there was anything we needed, anything it could do to make our lives easier, and we eventually said an ultrasound.

Jenny wasn't sure about this. The chance was remote, but what if the test revealed a baby in distress? How could that be good for her hospitalized husband? But she could tell the test was important to me. I wanted to know she and the baby were healthy, and I needed an uplifting something, a piece of unalloyed good news. On this morning, here it was, a photo of my second child, now eight weeks along, too soon to know the flavor, but here it was.

I've always known Jenny is strong. But consider what the ultrasound photo really said. It said that in addition to coping with a spouse whose head was haywire, mulling an offer from CNN made while she was on the train to my bedside, and keeping in touch with our firstborn who had now been whisked to my sister's in Boston and whom she dearly missed, Jenny was going to have to ride through my crisis while taking care of herself and the new life in her belly. Carlo Angelo Cruz, one of my nurses, called her the "superwoman."

She wound up as a cop, too.

"She had to field the most incredible succession of people coming in and out of that room," Mom remembers, "trying to make just the right balance between having him know that people were concerned but not having him completely swamped."

So many visitors reached Room 284 of the ICU that chairs wound up grouped around my bed like I was a fire pit providing warmth. Mika and Joe came until they had to go back to New York; Mom and Dad came every day; my sister, Stephanie, and my best friend, Marc, came; and NBC types. My senior staff—Alex Korson, Pete Breen, and Ann Edelberg—all came, too. Marc thought, illness or not, I wasn't really off the job at all. The job was coming to me. But the laughter was therapeutic, even if laughing made my head hurt even more.

Phil Griffin came with a gift, an iPad stocked with apps to kill time. Dr. Deshmukh came every day to see how I was doing. He didn't know I'd done a guest stint on the Sunday MJ and wasn't thrilled when he found out months later. Fairly often, my nurse Carlo helped to keep my muscles in shape by walking with me, first within the room for a few steps, then out in the hall. And one glorious day near the end, one of my other nurses, Elisa Weiss, got permission to take me downstairs in my wheelchair and out the very emergency-room doors I had walked in that first terrible Wednesday. For a couple of minutes, parked outside, Elisa, Jenny, and I basked in the sun and inhaled the smells of spring. It was the first time I had been out of the building, and I felt enormously buoyed, like I might be in the homestretch. Thank you, Elisa.

Both of my families, the one from 30 Rock and the one I spend holidays with, all the people I loved, had come together to help, which filled my painful head with much cheer. Mika introduced herself to my mother as "Chris's other mommy." And I could tell Dad was very proud his son knew all these high-flying NBC people. He and Mom watch *Morning Joe* but they had never come to the set. Mika, Joe, the president of MSNBC, everybody, here to see Chris? Impressive.

Much of the time, though, it was only Jenny and me.

I can't recall spending as much quality time. It was togetherness, sponsored by crisis. The brain bleed reaffirmed all those reasons we had married but that a workweek can overshadow. We talked about Andrew, who was too young to get on the phone with me, and we took trips down nostalgia highway. "Stupid stuff," Jenny says. We are *Law & Order* fans, and watched reruns. The ordinariness was the beauty.

Gradually, thoughts budded about what was going on at *MJ*. I asked for the BlackBerry. Had to check the ratings. I was feeling better.

No self-pity was shared between Jenny and me. Do not picture a weeping wife slumped across her beloved husband's hospital bed as the couple laments The Fates that have done this to their happy existence. Even in the dark days after I got home, no wailing about how this was unfair ever passed my lips. To sit passively and bemoan bad luck solves nothing. I deal with the hand that's been dealt. I don't waste time wishing for other cards.

Nor did Jenny and I discuss what my illness might mean for our future. Certainly we had no conversations about dying, because neither of us thought I would. Death was a possibility, yes, but only in the way it is when you board an airplane. Instead, most of the time, I wondered where I would wind up on the scale of possible lasting effects. We concentrated on getting out of there and going back to New York and having BLT and getting back to normal. I wanted normal, whatever normal was going to be.

One day at the hospital, Jenny's cell phone rang. The screen said UNKNOWN NUMBER.

"Hello?"

"Jenny?"

"Yes?"

"Joe Biden."

Just like that. No secretary intervening. Him.

"Oh. Hello, Mr. Vice President."

Cell-phone reception in the ICU was chronically bad, and now Jenny was terrified of losing the call, because how do you call back "unknown number"? The signal at the moment was good. She froze in place and listened because, as you might have heard, Joe Biden is a great talker.

He told her I was going to be fine. The doctor was great. The hospital was great. And, of course, he was living proof I would be great. He had survived what I had. Yes, the not knowing and the waiting were difficult, he said, but don't worry.

Thankfully, he didn't do what many well-wishers did, which was adopt a commiserating persona and say ever-so-sincerely that my situation was oh-so-terrible and oh-my-God how you doing? Instead, Biden made us feel the bind we were in was nothing, a blip.

Another day, Jeff Zucker showed up. He was the boss of all my bosses, the president and CEO of NBC Universal. Quickly, I morphed from hospital patient to loyal and hardworking employee. Mika and Joe's blitz on my behalf might have started to ease my fears about work, but this visit still required major game face. Zucker's The Guy.

Can't wait to get back, I told him, which wasn't true. I could wait, quite a bit longer. I added it was so annoying that the TV in my hospital room didn't carry MSNBC so I could watch my show and not miss an important thing. In other words: Jeff, I am practically not sick and the network is absolutely uppermost in my mind, not this pool of blood coating my brain.

Zucker read this for what it was: nonsense.

We've all heard people say nothing is more important than health. But when they say that, it's more reflex than belief, and they often secretly think you're malingering.

Zucker is different. Years ago, he had come close to dying from colon cancer. He had made the journey I was now making. He knew no job matters all that much, work is only what you do. He knew physical well-being is the prime directive.

He leaned in.

"Nothing is more important," he said. "Don't worry about anything. We've got it covered. We've got you covered."

Okay, I said.

He apparently didn't think he'd gotten through.

"Chris."

Pause.

"There's nothing more important."

He is a wise man. He helped me let go—let go of work—even more than I had.

The worst day, other than the first, was the Friday two days later. As Jenny sat with me, I tried to say something.

What came out was a kind of linguistic Cobb salad. Everything was there, but all tossed. "Bed, outside, window." Something like that.

Jenny could tell by my face that I knew my words were gibberish but she could also tell I couldn't self-correct. Did this herald a re-bleeding? Was this the anticipated spasm in advance of a stroke? Is this the descent?

I had had a bad night. Since the first day, nurses had been coming every hour or two and leading me through those familiar neurological tests designed to catch brain deterioration as early as possible, so the hospital could swing into action. Shrug your shoulders. Stick out your tongue. Close your eyes as tight as you can. I always passed.

"Who is the president of the United States?" a nurse said during one visit.

"You know," I said, joking, "we really don't know because we haven't seen his birth certificate."

Ha.

The tests did not cease at night, so my sleep was broken and battered, and on this Friday morning I had been surly. They had given me a drug and it had knocked me out, until I awoke speaking in tongues to Jenny.

She went in search of a nurse who quickly determined the villain was the drug, not my brain. But most of the time in the ICU, thoughts of a re-bleed or sudden dys-function hovered over the bed. Any minute I expected my vision would blur or my tongue would mangle a word. Why else would they be testing me constantly? I had had no warning in the back of the Escalade that morning. It seemed reasonable I'd get no warning the second time.

A re-bleed was not the only open question either.

Would there be brain surgery?

If an aneurysm was found during the coming second cerebral angiogram, my head would probably be opened up, though I didn't know that was Dr. Deshmukh's likely remedy. I only knew what he had said, that he'd go in and get it. Dad, however, knew brain surgery was a real possi-bility and he was worried, not because George Washington didn't know what it was doing, but because brain surgery is inherently delicate.

But at least it's definitive. Aneurysm found, aneurysm remedied. Case closed. Go in peace, my son.

Not finding one, though, would leave an eternal mys-tery. Why had I bled? It would be like a game of Clue in which no murder suspect was ever found in any room with any weapon. Dad actually preferred this scenario, though, because he did not want a surgical expeditionary force walking around in my head.

On Wednesday, May 5, one week to the day after I had arrived in the emergency room, I was again wheeled to the cerebral angiogram suite. Once again they cut into my leg, ran the catheter, shot the dye, scanned the scans.

Once again, no aneurysm.

Odds were rising my bleed had been freakish. Dr. Deshmukh wanted a third cerebral angiogram in two weeks, but things looked all right at the moment. I had no signs, either, of any secondary impact from the released blood.

Sooner than had seemed possible on day one, I could go home.

The next day, NBC sent a car and driver, and Jenny and I piled into the backseat for the ride up Interstate 95, to New York and Andrew and the restoration of our life, or at least the beginning of the restoration of our life. Some mastery was coming back to me. I felt good, or as good as you can with a headache that was now eight days old.

The hospital gave me do's and don'ts as we got ready to leave. Don't drive. Don't exercise. Don't do anything that raises blood pressure. Do take the antispasm pills. But nothing was said about how to deal with my emotions. I left George Washington University Hospital never having dealt with a topic certainly worthy of some major consideration.

What had sudden, random, life-threatening illness done to me?

Not to my body. Me.

In the car, I'm pretty sure I put my sad head in Jenny's lap.

chapter thirteen

An Angry Man

One of Dr. Deshmukh's instructions was no work.

No chance of that.

Upon arriving at our eighteenth-floor apartment on the Upper West Side on Thursday, May 6, I had an emotional—on my end, anyway—reunion with Andrew, who did not seem fazed his father had been away. MJ takes me out of town quite a bit. Andrew is used to absences, though having both parents away for so long was beyond our norm. If he had not been glad to see me or had been confused as to who I was, that would have been a dagger in my tired heart.

I then retreated to the living-room couch, where I largely stayed for the duration of the mend, mainlining television. To the doorman of our building, to the driver from Washington or anyone else, I must have looked like crap because I felt like it. My head remained hostile, though meds helped. On top of that, my hips hurt. They had been hurting before my event, maybe because of jogging I had been doing, but they hurt even more now.

In the coming days, it was obvious my son and I couldn't play as we usually did, because I had no gas for extended romps. I wasn't sleeping well. Moving about was a chore, although that first day at home I did get up to take a shower, my first since the Civil War. At the hospital, they had only sponge-bathed me, so a complete self-rinse was delightful, because I controlled the shampoo, I controlled the soap, and I controlled the duration.

Meals began arriving at our door. Phil Griffin sent lasagna the first night, and while it was heaven to no longer be eating hospital fare, the deliveries were so rich they could not possibly be good for a patient who had been told no exercise. I forced myself.

CNN had told Jenny to take all the time off she wanted to take care of me. She delivered an antispasm pill every two hours, even through the night, which meant she didn't get steady sleep either, probably not a good thing for BLT. We watched a lot of TV and many movies. I watched MJ a couple of times, only to see little things I would have done differently or not done at all. It was like sitting in the backseat while someone else drives your car. I could do nothing about them from the apartment, so I stopped watching.

More get-well cards came. So did more e-mails from Joe Scarborough. He never called while I was home, and I think I know why. If he had, I might have done what I did with Zucker. I might have faked good health and boundless enthusiasm. He avoided the charade by sending little missives that required only that I enjoy his concern.

How you feeling this morning?
Call if you need anything at all!
Call me if I can help in any way.

The worry of a second event was there, even though the medical chance of one was very small. My brain had been CAT-scanned, MRI'd, and cerebral-angiogrammed so thoroughly that I had much more reason to believe I was aneurysm-free than, for example, you do. Your gray matter has not been repeatedly swept electronically for possible mines.

But worry about that second event was not a matter of reason. Mika recalls how she hated this period when I seemed to be recovering but when I could be struck down again. "It was not over when it was over," she says.

A week after I got home, an e-mail arrived as I talked

with Phil, who had called to check on the patient. It was from someone at NBC's human resources department.

Hope this e-mail finds you well and improving, it said. *So happy to hear you are home. I just wanted to follow up that we have not received any information regarding your leave and wanted to remind you that you need to call the disability center.*

Disability center?

I am disabled?

I am not disabled.

Like *aneurysm* a couple of weeks earlier, the word was a punch.

The story seemed to be that anyone absent from work more than a certain number of days—and I was coming close—must be classified as "disabled," which apparently has something to do with which pot of money pays the handicapped employee. Until now, everyone had worked so hard to make my illness as easy to navigate as possible. Now I had to do paperwork? It just felt cold. Bloodless.

I called human resources and asked whether it wouldn't make more sense for me to skip the whole disability-center thing and use vacation days to cover the ones I had missed and would continue to miss. I'd worked for NBC for fifteen years and had mountains of untouched vacation days, because work routinely kept me from taking them all. But human resources was adamant. My records had to reflect what had happened. If I got sick again and missed many more days, they said, I'd regret not having duly noted the illness in the books and had the proper accounts charged.

I had to be marked disabled.

The paperwork was annoying. The message was worse. For the first time, my illness wasn't a crisis only within my circle of colleagues and family. It was an NBC thing, a matter of corporate record. Somewhere in some database, a box was being checked.

Disabled: Licht

The always healthy, perpetually energetic, no-setbacks employee was getting a blemish. And aren't people who are on disability simply gaming the system? Isn't that what people would think?

A few days later, a thick packet arrived with forms and explanations about COBRA and who was paying my salary, NBC or the state of New York. It might seem implausible, but that packet and all the stuff about disability pushed me through a psychological barrier and into a confrontation at last with the meaning of what I was going through.

Before, in the hospital, I had been in attack formation, participating in the hunt to find the source of my problem and guarding against its side effects. We had immediate goals, such as passing whatever the tests of the day were, and we had a long-range one, getting out of there and going home. Visitors descended daily. Doctors came daily. Meals and medicine were brought. The ICU is a twenty-four-hour place, never closed. I was occupied and diverted.

Upon discharge, this bustle had left my life. Each day now was fairly uneventful. Usually, it was my wife and son and I in the quiet of our apartment, and I had instructions to do nothing but relax as we awaited one more trip to Washington for a third cerebral angiogram, which would either find nothing and I could get more serious about returning to work, or find an aneurysm, which would delay me even more as they repaired it and I recovered.

I had time to think, in other words. That's what the disability e-mail and the health packet triggered. Thinking. And not of the good kind.

By now, I had more data about the severity of aneurysms than I had in the hospital. One reason was someone named Bret Michaels, an actor, director, and most famously a singer with the heavy-metal band Poison. A few days before my event, he had suffered exactly what I had, a massive headache followed by a diagnosis of subarachnoid hemorrhaging. I had been reading stories about his hospitalization, and there were many, because Michaels is a lot more famous than the executive producer of *MJ*.

Sprawled on the couch or lying in bed during these days, I began to get upset at the mysterious thing in my head that was now rendering me the disabled guy on an NBC form. I went over and over the past couple of weeks. Dad had warned that after getting home, I might get depressed. This wasn't that. This was anger. I tried to calm myself by saying it could have been a lot worse. After all, I had only wound up with headaches, not handicaps.

That cheery tack did no good. It had the opposite effect.

Wait. This could have been a lot *worse. This fucking thing could have taken me out.*

I got madder still at my head's defection from its normal state. For me, anger is not something to be endured passively, but to act upon. Its cause must be confronted. Blame must be apportioned. There must be an outcome.

Who or what was responsible for my near-death experience?

Where can I unload this anger, so I can feel better?

I had been told aneurysms more or less happen. If you smoke or use drugs, your risk is greater, or if you have high blood pressure, or if several people in your family have had one. But none of that applied to me.

Did I become sick, then, because of my lifestyle choices, like living in New York or enjoying a glass of wine with dinner? Was my home next to a landfill or beneath utility lines and my body had been poisoned or zapped, leading to a bulging artery? Did I consume massively caloric meals? Drive fast cars? Indulge in cocaine?

No, none of that. I was innocent.

Were Mom and Dad to blame for passing down aneurysm DNA?

No, they hadn't.

Was it the job, the television industry, that did this?

Lots of people assume stress was involved. But Dr. Deshmukh had told me stress does not cause arteries to inflate into aneurysms.

Nothing I had done caused this flaw in my brain. Nobody had done anything to me. Mine was the worst kind of anger. It came without a release valve.

My thinking spiraled.

It was a Jimmy Stewart sort of spiral, as in *It's a Wonderful Life*, which is a corny analogy, but I did begin to imagine what the world would have been like without me.

I had always envisioned a certain woman with certain characteristics coming into my life and then she had, and her name was Jenny. We were going to have a Norman

Rockwell sampler of kids, sports, and family gatherings. Andrew and I would play catch. Andrew and I would do his homework. He would get married. Jenny and I would flow gently into old age.

My brain bleed nearly snuffed that.

I imagined Jenny as a single mom. She enjoys her job, but she prefers being at home. If I had died, she would have had no choice but to continue working to support herself and Andrew. She would have given birth to Baby Licht Two, a child I would never have seen, and she would have become a single mom with twice the parental responsibility.

I imagined how it would have been for Andrew if I had died in the hospital. He would have been at his aunt's house in Boston and they would have driven him back to New York, where he would have found only Jenny in our apartment from that day on, and he wouldn't understand why Daddy was gone for good. I wouldn't have been there to witness the make-your-heart-melt trick he has perfected of late. In veteran Manhattanite style, he throws his two-year-old arm skyward and yells, "Taxi!"

At *Vanity Fair*'s party following the White House Correspondents' Association dinner in 2009, I had a long conversation with a fellow Syracuse graduate, Taye Diggs, the Broadway and screen actor who is married to actress Idina Menzel. Taye and Idina were a few months away from being parents for the first time and Taye asked that night what fatherhood was like, because Andrew had been born a few months earlier. My answer was unoriginal. That made it no less felt.

I would kill for my son, I told Taye. I would never have killed anybody before, but if someone threatened my son now, I would do it. In the first minutes after his birth, they had handed Andrew to me, and as they tended to Jenny, it had been him and me alone in another room. I had made a promise.

"I will never let anything happen to you."

The brain bleed nearly made me a liar. I wouldn't have been there to ward off the bad things menacing him. My dad had been there for me in the hospital, but I almost wasn't there for Andrew.

As these thoughts swirled, my future as an executive producer never came up. I did not think about how my career as a player might have been buried with me. It's true that in the hospital I had concerns about getting back to work and whether Willie's statement would make me seem fragile. But now, at home, only Jenny and Andrew and BLT mattered. They were what I had almost lost, not NBC.

The producer in me wanted to find someone to reprimand, or an action to take, in response to my bleed. But my efforts went nowhere. In retrospect, I wonder if the anger was simply a way to mask a deep sadness.

I did not throw things. I did not yell. The contemplation of the true seriousness of my illness had no exterior manifestations. I sought no professional help. I told no one about any of this, not even Jenny, because I'm the family's protector and did not wish to seem weak in her eyes. I solve the family's problems. I don't become one. Jenny was already missing work for me and already serving as a nurse and I did not want to turn her into a shrink, holding the hand of a wimp of a husband.

But she knew.

chapter fourteen

A Walk and a Lunch

Mike Barnicle is both a classy guy and a regular one. He has a big heart and a big palette of passions, including politics, baseball, and Boston, where he lives. As I've said, he was born and raised in newspapers. He doesn't have much use for journalists who sit in offices and do Google searches and call this reporting, instead of walking neighborhoods and meeting actual humans and talking with them. He is a man of rich and diverse connections whom I admire greatly.

When Mike comes to New York to do *MJ*, which is often, NBC puts him up at a hotel near Central Park, and he tries to take a daily walk of nearly five miles around it. One day not long after I got home from the hospital, perhaps the day the disability packet arrived from NBC, he asked me to join him for one of his strolls. I was a long way from robust, but I decided to hobble along at least partway, and the day was gorgeous and the park was in May bloom.

As we ambled from my building on Central Park West and down the sidewalks, Mike chattered about delightfully insignificant things. This, that, his broken BlackBerry, and how he was getting it fixed. He didn't know my mental state and I didn't tell him. No matter. I liked his company and liked being out, because I hardly had been out at all. My strength didn't last long, and as we reached the point where Seventy-second Street meets the park and prepared to part, he turned to me.

"You really have to appreciate how lucky you are," he said. "You're able to see how loved you are without having to die."

He sensed his words didn't register as much as he had hoped. He gently nudged me again: You have great support, Chris. You're lucky to know that.

Mike had visited me at the hospital in Washington, and had suggested then that perhaps my hemorrhage wasn't an all-bad event, because it would reorder my priorities a bit. He really thought I was too intense about work. With or without me, he had said at GW, there was going to be television. There was going to be a *Morning Joe*. But there was only one me and I needed to take care of myself. He urged me to revel in my good fortune. What if my bleed had happened when the show was in still-battered New Orleans a few weeks earlier, instead of in Washington, mere minutes from one of the great neurological departments in the country?

At the corner of Seventy-second, Mike didn't turn all this into a lecture. He spoke but a few words and was done.

"I'll see you later," he said, and walked off with his newspaper.

Mike had been a very close friend of Tim Russert, NBC's Washington bureau chief who had died two years before. I had been moved then by how he had helped the Russert family get through his death, and remember how Peggy Noonan, a *Wall Street Journal* columnist, had written that the standard by which each of us should be measured is whether we wind up as beloved as Russert had been.

Mike had a point. People had been wonderful during my crisis. I hadn't expected it. And I had been lucky, indeed. Our walk in the park, coming during my days of silent anger about nearly dying and having no one to punish, made me think there was, after all, some good here, the love of other people, not the least of them Mike.

Three days or so after the walk, I met Joe for brunch, the first time I had seen him since Washington. E-mail had been an okay way for us to stay in touch if the topic was my health, but not if it was work. If I passed my third cerebral angiogram in a few days, I would be on a glide path back, and that meant I needed to know in depth what had been happening at 30 Rock and what he was thinking.

As we ate at a restaurant in New York called P.J. Clarke's, Joe mentioned that Mika had scolded him for using only e-mails and not phone calls to stay in touch with me at home.

No, I said, your e-mails were perfect.

Throughout, he and Mika had shown so much concern, making me feel so much better. There was no more appropriate moment to tell him, even if such a naked expression of gratitude might make a very private man uncomfortable.

No matter what happens, I told Joe, even if we have fights, even if my contract is not renewed and I leave *MJ* for some reason, "I will never forget what you did for me."

I got teary.

"I will never forget," I said again.

He suggested I shouldn't have been so surprised.

"Of course I love you," he said.

Which I now knew beyond doubt.

On Friday, May 21, still feeling angry but perhaps not quite as much after talking with Mike and Joe, I took the train to Washington, looking to put a period at the end of a sentence. Jenny came, too, of course. I could have had this third angiogram done by someone in New York, but I trusted Dr. Deshmukh and the hospital, and no other institution could possibly have treated us as well.

Once again, I was taken to the angiogram suite and a catheter went into my leg and all the way through me, and the peering at monitors began. Once again, Jenny waited.

She was very nervous. If an aneurysm was found, after having eluded Dr. Deshmukh for more than three weeks, I would be devastated, she feared, demoralized. It wouldn't mean death or an inability to speak or anything like that, but it would mean more doctors and tests, more invasion of me in an effort to eliminate the now-found aneurysm, more hospital time, perhaps days of recovery, pushing normalcy further away.

But if my arteries were clean for a third time, all the statistics suggested my brain would not rear up again, that my event had been a rogue. It might have been merely a vein that leaked, not an artery. Being under less pressure, veins are less troublesome if they bleed. Or it might have been an aneurysm so very tiny it was simply not visible, that it had bled and sealed itself completely and was not a candidate for future bleeding.

The test finished. Dr. Deshmukh looked at me.

My brain was fine. No more tests were necessary. No more cutting into my leg. No more doctors.

Go to work if you wish, Dr. Deshmukh said.

I wished.

"You can consider this event behind you," he said.

Well, in a physical sense I could.

$$\left[\text{chapter fifteen} \right]$$

Back

Twenty-six days after my brain popped, I walked down the stairs of a subway entrance near my apartment and joined the Monday-morning crush on a southbound train, emerging a few minutes later at Rockefeller Center.

I don't usually ride the subway to 30 Rock, not because I shun the masses, but because *Morning Joe* begins so early NBC sends a car to make sure I get there. Coming out of the subway flooded me with sensations I hadn't felt in a month. Thousands of workers pounded toward their offices, side-stepping one another on the sidewalks, buzzing on phones, noshing bagels, lining the low marble walls of the plazas on Sixth Avenue to read for a few minutes with their coffees.

The cacophony and energy were soothing. I was back among the living, feeling the pulse of the city. I bought a coffee, too.

On this first possible day I could return after Deshmukh's green light, May 24, I was easing back. I wasn't running the day's *MJ*, which was nearly finished by the time I got there. But for days now, my eagerness to rejoin the team had grown as my headache faded, even if I was still secretly fencing with bigger issues.

Jenny didn't quite understand why I was going back right then. Nobody was pressuring me, or her, so she assumed we would have weeks of family time, at least more than the few we had had. But we hadn't been doing much. By going back to work, I wasn't abandoning idyllic days of museum tours and leisurely lunches; I hadn't been up for things like that. At least by getting off the couch and going back to work I would be productive. I missed Control Room 3A. I wasn't going back as a heroic statement of awesome dedication to the National Broadcasting Company. Television is what I love. The job was never a labor, and the sooner I went back the greater my morale would be and the healthier I would feel.

Besides, even if I had waited weeks more to return, Jenny knew there was never a chance I was going to quit outright after my illness and turn toward a life of monastic chanting or buy a cozy place above San Diego and tend llamas and support the legalization of marijuana. "He would be miserable," she says.

That first morning, I sat, not in the executive producer's chair, but one seat over as Pete Breen, who had been running the show during the past weeks, took the team through the final minutes. During a commercial, they turned on the 3A camera, so Mika and Joe and everybody on the set could see that although Elvis had left the building in April, he was back now, whole and alert.

There was a mountain of mail on my desk. After the show, I started sifting it, enjoying the leisurely routine of it. My BlackBerry had only one appointment, lunch with Phil Griffin. I had been hoping to come back below radar, but word soon spread beyond the *MJ* family and into the rest of the building, because journalists can never keep any news to themselves.

Of course, everybody wanted to hear the story.

What did it feel like, Chris? Where were you when the pain started? Were you scared? And Jenny was pregnant during this? Biden was involved?

I love telling the story because it *is* quite a story, and I'm aware that the contrast between what I had been—healthy and young—and what happened to me leads almost everyone to ponder the possibility of random death. I am both a cautionary tale and a lottery winner, and fascinating either way.

Quite a few people treated me as gingerly as a Wedg-
wood plate. The MJ family knew I hadn't suffered any neurological tics. But others knew only what the rumor mill
had churned up or what Willie had said on the air, and
not knowing much about aneurysms, assumed I was now a
child to be spoken to slowly and loudly.

"Helllooooo, Chris. How arrrre you?"

Some seemed surprised I was vertical. They had never
expected to see me alive and intact again. They would tell
me to take it easy, as if without their wise counsel I would
be pondering an Iron Man competition. If I was still at the
office in midafternoon in those first few days, they would ask
why I still was. I began to think they were worried I would
start bleeding again right in front of them, and they would be
blamed as my face hit the tile in a spectacular dive of death.

Still others thought my intensity was the cause of my
near miss. Chris is volcanic, see, and his brain exploded.
He paid the price. Be quiet around him.

None of this made me mad, or at least any madder
than I already was about what the brain bleed had nearly
done. I didn't say anything to people about their assump-
tions or their clumsy advice. It wasn't worth getting upset
over. In time, people in the building would see my skills
were still there, my decision making sound, and maybe

even find out that aneurysms do not grow inside the brain because you happen to be type A.

That first day, Phil Griffin took me to lunch at a sushi place. The president of MSNBC had been shaken by my illness in a way that had nothing to do with any problems my absence created or threatened to create for one of the network's best shows. It made him feel vulnerable, as it probably makes everyone feel. He never asked in so many words at lunch, but I sensed he was curious how I saw the world now, not as an executive producer, but as a person. How was I different?

My answer was a plug for myself, which might have been smarmy but it does show that the brain bleed has killed none of my desire to be a player. In fact, it heightened it, as I now told Phil.

Bigger things. I want to do bigger things, I told him.

The message wasn't that I was itching to leave *MJ*. Hardly. I merely wanted Phil to know that not only had illness not finished me, I hoped to be even more of a player at the network, have a bigger role.

In my business, young talent is often told something like this: Wait your turn. Don't try to get it all at once. Don't overreach. Put your head down, work, good things will come to you. Be patient.

But what if you don't have unlimited time to wait as the line slowly moves and you inch toward the front? What if you carefully map a five-year plan but don't get five years, because an aneurysm gets you in three? My brain bleed was an official public notice that no one can count on having the time they expect. If you're ready and capable, reach for the next level of whatever you do. If something looks appealing and challenging, have a go. Otherwise, it's a pretty average life.

I haven't wandered so far into the realm of cliché that I now have a bucket list—win Iditarod, excavate Mayan ruins, stomp grapes—but I'm far more open to spontaneity. You sometimes hear that illness is a way of telling the victim to slow down. That's not the message my illness sent me. Mine said, "Get moving."

At the end of that first, low-key day back, I went home and crashed. I was surprised by how exhausted I felt. But by Tuesday, June 1, it was me in the EP's chair as *Morning Joe* began. There was no way my return would pass without formal recognition on the air. I knew they would inflict something upon me, but figured Mika and Joe would do no more than ask that the control-room camera be turned on so the audience would know I was back and I could wave. Oh, they did much worse.

Without telling me, they had lined up Dr. Deshmukh as a guest, as well as the chief operating officer of the hospital, Kimberly Russo. They ordered me to come out of Control Room 3A, march down the hall, and sit with them on the set, on the air, no makeup, no prep. If you see the video, I look uncomfortable, because there is always a risk that this kind of thing comes across as self-indulgent. At least I knew which cameras to look at.

"Awwwww, he's back," Mika said, "and I'm so glad for so many reasons. Do you remember that morning?"

"Yup," Joe said.

"Yeah, I do, too," she said, slightly miffed.

Joe realized she was making a joke.

"Oh, is this the blame Joe thing? Is this the blame Joe thing?"

They were referring to how, on that day in Washington, Joe had gotten irritated at my inability to get him the camera angle he wanted, and minutes later I had commenced a brain bleed, as if his irritation and my event were cause and effect, even though they weren't.

Explain what the bleed was like, Mika said to me.

"To say it was the worst headache of my life doesn't really describe it," I said, "because it was like nothing I ever felt before."

"You looked horrible," Mika said.

"Thank you," I said.

Dr. Deshmukh told the audience I was in that mysterious class of cases for which no cause for the bleeding is found. But my prognosis was good, he said.

Aside from what they had done for me on that first frightening day, the segment was the best gift Mika and Joe could have given, because it showed I was fine in every way and it made me feel so normal to be back and teasing with them. A blogger wrote: *Licht Looks Mah-ve-lous in* Morning Joe *Return*. Some e-mailers kidded that because Mika and Joe were talking with the big guest, the show had blown right through its scheduled break at the top of the hour, which would not have happened if I were where I belonged, in the control room. I even got a welcome-back e-mail from the West Wing of the White House.

Yes, I was back.

"I'm back," I said.

That's not the same as cured.

chapter sixteen

On the Deck

Years ago, my parents bought a vacation house in Charlestown, Rhode Island, about a tenth of a mile from the beach. You can see the Atlantic Ocean from it. In the summer, Mom and Dad like to lend the house to me for a week and to my sister for one, so we can each bring our families in solitude and chill out, though in the past I often did not stay for the entire week because work got in the way.

Now, sitting out on the deck of the house sometime during the first days after returning to 30 Rock, I was watching Andrew play. I had my laptop out and was Web-surfing to no purpose but diversion. My heart filled as I looked at my son. Here was an entirely good thing, my little man playing, with nothing more on his plate than fun, overlooking the ocean on a late spring day. The gulf between the sweet scene and the anger I had been toting was vast.

Families of crime victims often say they have forgiven the creep who killed their husband or teenage daughter, because anger creates nothing good. I had always laughed at the monumental absurdity of that. Anger is not always a useless emotion. In that situation, my anger would have a worthy target: the killer. It would have a point, making sure he feels the sting of justice.

But no criminal suspect caused my event. I had gone down the checklist of possible culprits and my anger at nearly dying had nowhere to go. It could never be directed at anything, no matter how much I wished otherwise or how long I held on to it. I would only be able to sit on the deck and stay mad, and then go home to New York and stay mad, and then go to work and stay mad. I would roam like Ahab, endlessly searching for someone or something to blame for having brushed way too close to the end.

I kept sitting there, thinking in the spring breezes.

Or, on the other hand, I could accept the futility of this. As I more or less had told Phil, a life-threatening illness alters how you look at clocks. Did I wish to use up more of my life's limited minutes being furious? Or stop that and start enjoying Andrew and the rest of my days? There is only one rational option, isn't there? And so, as my son played, I exercised a mental muscle I didn't know

I had and told myself something akin to what I had said inside the MRI machine that first night at the hospital.

Enough. Done.

My event had been brutal proof my life could end before today's sun sets at the beach, because the aneurysm could rupture again and I might not be as fortunate again. I was still young, but that was no guarantee that tomorrow would include me. I would not expend any more time staying angry at something I did not cause, that nobody caused and nobody could have stopped.

Still sitting on the deck, I kept following this thread of thought.

If I could do that, if I could no longer be mad at almost dying, then logically how could I get mad at much lesser things that might happen to me, the things of daily life? If a videotape got messed up during MJ, that would not be the equivalent of having a brain bleed. It would not be worth eviscerating someone with an e-mail after the show. And if others thought I might now be a pushover of a producer, I couldn't help that. Let them think so and let them test me if they wish. It will be obvious to them soon enough I haven't lost any moves in Control Room 3A, or any passion for the show. I'll still push back.

If Joe and Mika got mad because we had a lousy guest

or their travel arrangements fell apart, that wouldn't be as serious as the fairly personal setback of having nearly died. It's okay if they're not totally happy about something on the show or not totally happy with me. It's okay if I take a day off or use all my vacation time or make more time for my family; I shouldn't worry what anyone will think. Besides, I knew now Mika and Joe were happy in a cosmic sense. In the emergency room of George Washington University Hospital, they had been in my trench. They had shown unconditional love for not just a colleague but a friend.

Watching my son play, I was accepting what I couldn't control, which is the ultimate act of control. People say all the time you should "let it go," whatever it is. A comment, an irritation, bad news of any sort. I wasn't used to doing that. I was used to counterpunching until the situation was reshaped to my satisfaction. Giving up illogical anger might still be giving up, but I realized that in this case that meant victory.

I forgave my brain.

I left the deck happier. Throughout my illness, I had worried about where I would end up on the damaged scale, but I had never really allowed for the possibility I might end up better off in some ways. My epiphany about letting go of the anger about what had happened might seem pat, too neat, but clarity can descend like that, under the right conditions. These had been perfect. Andrew was the catalyst, though he did not know it. He couldn't even spell it. But simply by being there, playing so sweetly, my boy helped his daddy put away not only a brain bleed, but a lot of nonsense.

chapter seventeen

The Meaning of Time

My illness started not too far from the U.S. Naval Observatory. It ended there, too.

For some time, I had been struggling with how to thank Joe Biden for what he had done during my brain bleed, from taking Mika's call in those first hours to calling Dr. Deshmukh to cheering up Jenny and me by cell phone. I wanted to write him a letter, a suitably formal way to convey my gratitude.

The vice president was having a lawn party for journalists at the Observatory, his official residence in Washington, and Joe, Mika, and I were invited. I e-mailed Biden's press office to ask if it would be appropriate to hand him the letter I had in mind and was told it would be. But I couldn't finish the thing, not the way I wanted. All my attempts came out too saccharine, way over-the-top.

Just tell him, Jenny said.

Joe and Mika, it turned out, couldn't attend the party but I still wanted to go. So on Saturday, June 5, Jenny and I stood in a receiving line at the vice president's house. One of Biden's staffers recognized me, perhaps because he had seen me on television. Then it was our turn to be introduced to this man who had leaped into my crisis.

For a brief second, I could tell Biden couldn't place my name.

"You saved my life," I said.

And from the data banks of the thousands of people he knows and all the events he has been a part of, he remembered and greeted me as if we had shared my brain bleed. He remembered everything. The usual thirty-second photo opportunity gave way to five minutes of reminiscing as the line backed up.

"I can't thank you enough," I said.

He hugged me. He hugged Jenny. He said he had been so worried. He is a great and kind person, and the photo taken that day of Jenny and me being embraced by the vice president of the United States will live on in our family forever. My children will be able to tell their friends that in the worst moment of Daddy's life, a busy public official put aside the important things he was doing to help.

Among my family and colleagues, there are doubts that this nearly dying business has changed me all that much or will. Mom is among them. Dad, too. Take more vacation days? They don't believe it. Work still looms too large, they say. They predict I'll be enjoying a week at the Rhode Island house and Joe will call and I'll be gone, off on some mission.

Even Jenny says I haven't changed as much as she expected or hoped. She thought I would feel I had been granted that classic second chance at life and would pare the hours worked on weekends and inflate family time.

I am, though, getting there. Watch, Mom. I'll take all my vacation. I know now how important it is to make more mental space for family. I know now I shouldn't have been on the phone as they took Andrew for his circumcision, because whatever I was discussing couldn't have been significant. I know I shouldn't have gone back to work right after he was born, or skipped my friend's wedding because it was Sweeps Week. I know you can't give 100 percent to work, because there's no percentage left for anything else.

Few of us can pivot on a dime. Just because I had a moment of clarity on the deck about how futile and wasteful it can be to get angry doesn't mean I never will. I'll have to train myself, remind myself, to distinguish the moments worthy of anger from those that are not. I'm sure I'll fail now and then. Re-jiggering my behavior and attitudes is a project that will take the rest of my life.

But in many small ways I'm already a different man. When my anger was greatest about what my brain bleed nearly took from me, I didn't think of NBC. I thought of Jenny and Andrew. And when, on December 7, BLT entered the world as Ryan Christopher Licht, I took my full paternity leave from *Morning Joe*, perhaps a small step for you but a big one for me.

These days, I call home more than I used to, just to see how Jenny is. I wouldn't have thought it possible to think any more highly of her than I did, but I do. Maybe even she didn't realize what a steel core she has. Pregnant, juggling a job offer, given at other times to high flying emotion, she put everything aside and went more Mika than Mika to make sure I came out all right.

Dad and I are vastly closer. It was always easier to read Mom, who's outgoing by nature. Dad was less demonstrative. But to see him in the hospital talking with my doctors and monitoring the fine print of my care, I realized I had the perfect, medically skilled, loving patient advocate. He was deeply shaken by what happened to me. Before, we'd talk once in a while. Now, all the time.

At work, I've noticed that when someone asks me a question or presents an issue for decision, I don't answer as quickly and dismissively as I used to. A second or two ticks by. I consider the question. I consider them. I think it throws people off, though I'm not trying to do that. Maybe it's because, after their incredible e-mails and cards and phone calls during my illness, my colleagues are more real to me now. Maybe I have less tunnel vision about the world in which I walk every day. I give verbal hugs more than ever. At the postmortems after every *Morning Joe*, I say less and let my leadership team say more because I don't need to have my finger in every pie all the time.

True, Mr. BlackBerry and I are as entwined as ever. What might be hard to grasp is that a life-threatening illness didn't make me care about *Morning Joe* any less. Quite the opposite. It's more fun. I can go to Control Room 3A knowing there are worse things than whether people get mad at me, worse things than whether someone doesn't push a microphone button on time, and more important things than whether I'm being included in everything Joe and Mika are doing.

Joe has an expression: "Scared money never wins." It means, simply, play with confidence. Believe in yourself. My decisions come easier now and they're clearer. Options are weighed on their merits without calculating the politics. I don't pick fights anymore, which doesn't mean I run from them. But I don't seek out conflict to prove I'm The Man.

On the air the other day, Joe was tweaking then-Governor Tim Pawlenty of Minnesota, a potential candidate for the Republican presidential nomination in 2012, for not coming on the show in a while. But Pawlenty had already agreed to come on the show the very next week. Joe didn't know that, nor did I, so I had no reason to get in Joe's ear and correct the undeserved slam while we were still live.

We looked like cheap-shot kings. But I did not excoriate the person who forgot to tell us about Pawlenty's booking. Back in the day, I would have. I would have petulantly sought to ruin her day for ruining mine. To no good end, of course.

In late fall 2010, there occurred a sad, astounding coincidence. When I worked at my first job in Allentown, a woman named Denise Cramsey was one of the producers at our company. Denise had, in fact, trained me. But I had largely lost track of her until we bumped into each other at a party, when *Morning Joe* visited Los Angeles a few months after my brain bleed.

Like me, Denise had gone on to do much bigger things

in television, receiving multiple Emmy nominations and winning twice. At the party in L.A., she had raced across the room to give me a warm greeting, a big hug and her card, and when I got back to New York, she was one of the old acquaintances I had made a point of finding time to e-mail, to say we needed to get together again. She was forty-one, a couple of years older than me. She, too, was a graduate of Syracuse.

Two days before Thanksgiving, Denise collapsed and died of a brain aneurysm.

Rarely have I felt such chills. Her death transported me right back to April, and how close I'd come indeed.

When I get a head twinge now, there's always a microsecond of wonder about whether it's all happening again. It passes quickly, and I realize this is a normal headache, the kind we all get. I will probably always wonder whenever that happens. There are other reminders of my bleed, too. One day, NBC sent a benefit form to executives. One section told us to check a box if we had been absent from work for more than five days in a row in the last year.

I checked.

If you've checked, it said, explain.

"Subarachnoid hemorrhage."

Never had to confess such a flaw, ever. But I don't, and

won't, fear a second event. Such worry about the unknowable is pointless.

On that day in April, at the moment Dr. Mayersak said the CAT scan had found blood, I knew my life would be different, but I never imagined it would become what it has. I hope you never hear a doctor say anything as frightening to you or anyone you love. But I am so much smarter now. I am so much more confident. I feel at peace. A hole in my head wound up cutting the knot in my stomach. Isn't that bizarre, to come so close to leaving the premises and wind up new and improved?

But it's simple, really. What can they, anybody, do to me? Nothing can be worse than what nearly happened. Being fired was always my greatest fear, because I loved *Morning Joe* and wanted to remain a part of it. Now, if they boot me out, I will find another job in television somewhere and I'll be okay, because I'll be alive. And in the unlikely event I can't get a job in the business, that will be okay, too, for the same reason. I will take my two boys and my beautiful wife and we'll figure out something. I won't curl up in a ball and moan that nobody wants me. Maybe Jenny, the children, and I would go run a B&B in Vermont after all.

I never thought about dying before any of this. The

young rarely do, especially if their bodies have never been less than perfect. I think about it now, about how close death is for all of us, about how I dodged it and my friend Denise didn't, how I was lucky and she wasn't.

But my thoughts about death are not morbid. They're more useful. What happened to me was an unsolicited, but invaluable, reminder that none of us gets to choose how many days we have. Everybody's supply is limited, some far more than others. There are no hours to be wasted on anger at an illness that is not your fault. There are none to be wasted on anxiety about who says what about you or whether they like you. These things are beyond your power to influence. What you can control, though, is how you use the unknowable amount of time you have. And if you choose not to invest in the uncontrollable and the trivial, something wonderful happens. You actually wind up with more time: more to enjoy family and friends and colleagues, more to keep yourself sane, more to appreciate simply being here. It is a lesson underscored every time *Morning Joe* goes to Washington, because inevitably my daily shuttling around the capital takes me right past the entrance of the George Washington emergency room.

On Christmas Eve 2010, as we do every year, the Licht siblings and their families gathered with Mom and Dad at the house on the hill in Connecticut for a big dinner filled with wine and laughter. It is a tradition, kept in a journal, that we select the family's top ten events of the rapidly closing year, things like births and new jobs.

Winding up as the Event of the Year was a quirky sort of honor. But I was damn glad to be there to accept. It was time well spent.

chapter eighteen

So Zen

One September morn after my return, Phil Griffin shot me an e-mail even as *Morning Joe* was still on the air.

Not good, it said.

Phil was pissed about a conversation that had just taken place during the show, and he wanted to talk about it with me because, as executive producer, I'm responsible for what airs. Even so, being summoned to the front office to explain an on-air episode is so rare that I knew this e-mail was a bad omen. It was so rare that if I had gotten one like it before my brain popped, I know how the hours prior to talking with Phil would have gone.

My God, am I in trouble? What's gonna happen? How could the folks on the set have put me in this situation?

Dread would have chewed up more of my limited time on Planet Earth in calculations of possible recriminations, none of which I could do anything about, which would not have stopped the angst. I would have been frozen in my office until the phone call or the audience with Phil, at which time a head might roll and it wouldn't be his.

Here's what actually happened after I read Phil's summons.

In an e-mail, I acknowledged his request for a conversation. Then, after the show finished, I conducted the usual staff postmortem of the segments and guests. And I deposited the impending session with Phil into a brand-new, what-happens-happens vault, to be retrieved only when it was time for the conversation.

Then Joe called. He knew Phil had contacted me.

Don't freak out, Joe said.

He was envisioning a Woodstock of worry by Old Chris.

"Joe," I said, "I'm really not freaking out. I have plans today. I'm not going to stick around."

If I was in the building when Phil was ready for the conversation, I'd be there.

"You don't need to calm me down," I said.

Not having to reassure me meant Joe and Mika had one less thing to worry about during this flap, making things better for all.

The plans I had mentioned to Joe included a doctor's appointment, and I was waiting in the exam room that afternoon when Phil finally called for the big chat. The head of human resources for NBC was on the line with him, which is usually a leading indicator that someone's professional health is about to take a turn.

Phil asked if I had known what was going to happen on the set that morning. I hadn't, or at least I hadn't known the discussion was going to go the way it did.

What they did out there, Phil said, could get you in a lot of trouble.

Maybe. But I wouldn't disown them to cover myself, because they had been with me in the emergency room.

I knew Phil would be within his rights to suspend me. If he did and if my conduct became an issue in my contract negotiations, which were not far down the road, well, I could live with that, because what choice did I have? That was what I realized on the deck with Andrew, namely, the beauty of knowing when you have the power to change something and when you don't. I didn't want to be suspended and I love NBC, but you cannot enjoy a job, you cannot do it well, if you are always afraid of losing it. And I wasn't anymore.

In the end, my boss and friend didn't suspend me. I

might have lost points with Phil because of what happened on the air, but my day turned out exactly as it would
have if Old Chris had worried the whole time. I had spared
myself a lot of hand-wringing and been more productive
and emerged right where I would have anyway.

A few days later, I was supposed to go to Las Vegas—
for me, not the show. Las Vegas is perhaps my favorite
diversion and several friends and I have a sort of annual
guys' trip there. But this year, members of the posse had
been dropping out. Then, at the last minute, my friend
Marc, the only one besides me still going, canceled.

Jenny thought it would be kind of pathetic to go anyway. A grown man flying to Vegas alone to play the tables
alone and eat alone? Sad. But there was no way I was not
going. I do not put things off these days, another learned
lesson.

I could have told myself that, well, Marc has given me
an out and I can cancel the trip and keep working to make
up all those days I missed in the spring when I so thoughtlessly allowed blood to spill in my head.

But that scenario was not going to happen. I was going
to grab the days. So I said to me: Go. Go. Enjoy.

On a Friday morning, by myself, I headed to JFK for
a 7:45 flight to Las Vegas. It was raining so hard the ex-

pressways were flooded, and despite my clear suggestion of an alternate route, the driver decided he knew best. And drove us straight into a standstill. Not only was traffic stopped cold, it didn't move for three hours. Three hours. I missed my flight. I began trolling the airline schedule on my BlackBerry for the next one. I missed that one. My short vacation in Vegas was shrinking by the minute. This was worse than missing a flight for the show. This was cutting into *my* time, pool time in the warm sun.

This is where Old Chris traditionally rears his head, blisters the car's driver for wasting hours and hours of my short weekend getaway, screams at the airline, and yet, somehow, gets no closer to the airport for all that emotion. I didn't do any of that. Now let me be clear. I wasn't happy. But I consciously reminded myself not to overreact to a situation that had no remedy.

Rain? It happens.

Drivers who won't listen to a good suggestion? Happens.

Brain bleeds? Them, too.

From the car, I called Mom, to pass the time.

"You're so Zen," she said.

I got to Las Vegas. It gets better. After Marc had canceled on me, I had called Chris Marlin, the same friend whose wedding I skipped a while back, and lobbied him heavily to join me on this junket because I wanted time with a friend. He was too busy. Then, at the last second, Chris changed his mind, and now he, too, showed up in Las Vegas, flying all the way from the East Coast to eat a single dinner with an old friend.

What a great evening.

Acknowledgments

The idea for this book was not mine. It was the idea of my friend, and frequent *Morning Joe* guest, Jon Meacham. It was Jon who invited me to lunch last summer to tell me that it was important for me to tell my story. He even came up with the title at that lunch, knowing fully that I didn't yet have the answer to the question "What did I learn when I almost died?" He started me on the journey to find out, and I will always be grateful to him for pushing me to do the book and the faith he showed by bringing the idea to Simon & Schuster.

Speaking of Simon & Schuster, Jonathan Karp and Priscilla Painton have been incredibly supportive since the moment we met. Every step of the process, they've nurtured this book as if it was their own story.

This book would not exist without the tireless work of my collaborator and de facto therapist Steve Twomey. The many hours we spent together helped me absorb not only how the incident affected my life, but also the lives of those closest to me. What you have just read is the result of Steve taking the time to interview more than a dozen people connected to that day. He is not only a meticulous Pulitzer Prize–winning reporter, but also a skilled writer who captures my emotion and voice perfectly. He is also now a friend.

I would also like to thank everyone who took some of their valuable time to help me tell this story: Phil Griffin, Mike Barnicle, Willie Geist, and Farra Ungar from MSNBC, with a special thanks to Cate Cetta of MSNBC, for patiently juggling so many phone calls, e-mails, and appointments essential to making this book happen. From GWU Medical Center: Dr. Vivek Deshmukh, Dr. Ryanne Mayersak, Jenn Klemperer, Mike Hite, and Carlo Angelo Cruz. (I guess this would be as good a time as any to also thank them for saving my life.) Also, Marc Cadin, Lesley Sookram, and Jay Carney. And of course my best friend, who's never shy about telling me the truth and whom I believe is a psychiatrist largely because of our friendship, Marc Nespoli.

There are many people who made this book possible, but none more than Joe and Mika. Their support of this project from idea to completion never wavered. What we've built professionally and personally is unique and something I will always cherish. They are much more than colleagues. They are friends.

Finally, my family. When the you-know-what hits the fan, this is the team you'd want in your corner. Mom, Dad, and Stephanie: we've come out of this experience closer than ever.

And most of all, Jenny, who gave me two beautiful boys, Andrew and Ryan, and proved once again, I married the greatest woman in the world. I love you.